W9-AFV-808

Teach Yourself
VISUALLY™
Photoshop® CS2

Visual

by Mike and Linda Wooldridge

WILEY

Wiley Publishing, Inc.

Teach Yourself VISUALLY™ Photoshop® CS2

Published by
Wiley Publishing, Inc.
111 River Street
Hoboken, NJ 07030-5774

Published simultaneously in Canada

Copyright © 2005 by Wiley Publishing, Inc., Indianapolis, Indiana

No part of this publication may be reproduced, stored in a retrieval system or transmitted in any form or by any means, electronic, mechanical, photocopying, recording, scanning or otherwise, except as permitted under Sections 107 or 108 of the 1976 United States Copyright Act, without either the prior written permission of the Publisher, or authorization through payment of the appropriate per-copy fee to the Copyright Clearance Center, 222 Rosewood Drive, Danvers, MA 01923, (978) 750-8400, fax (978) 646-8600. Requests to the Publisher for permission should be addressed to the Legal Department, Wiley Publishing, Inc., 10475 Crosspoint Blvd., Indianapolis, IN 46256, (317) 572-3447, fax (317) 572-4355. Online: www.wiley.com/go/permissions.

Library of Congress Control Number: 2005923193

ISBN-13: 978-0-7645-8840-2

ISBN-10: 0-7645-8840-0

Manufactured in the United States of America

10 9 8 7 6 5 4 3 2 1

Trademark Acknowledgments

Wiley, the Wiley Publishing logo, Visual, the Visual logo, Teach Yourself VISUALLY, Read Less - Learn More and related trade dress are trademarks or registered trademarks of John Wiley & Sons, Inc. and/or its affiliates. Adobe and Photoshop are registered trademarks of Adobe Systems Incorporated. All other trademarks are the property of their respective owners. Wiley Publishing, Inc. is not associated with any product or vendor mentioned in this book.

Contact Us

For general information on our other products and services please contact our Customer Care Department within the U.S. at 800-762-2974, outside the U.S. at 317-572-3993 or fax 317-572-4002.

For technical support please visit www.wiley.com/techsupport.

LIMIT OF LIABILITY/DISCLAIMER OF WARRANTY: THE PUBLISHER AND THE AUTHOR MAKE NO REPRESENTATIONS OR WARRANTIES WITH RESPECT TO THE ACCURACY OR COMPLETENESS OF THE CONTENTS OF THIS WORK AND SPECIFICALLY DISCLAIM ALL WARRANTIES, INCLUDING WITHOUT LIMITATION WARRANTIES OF FITNESS FOR A PARTICULAR PURPOSE. NO WARRANTY MAY BE CREATED OR EXTENDED BY SALES OR PROMOTIONAL MATERIALS. THE ADVICE AND STRATEGIES CONTAINED HEREIN MAY NOT BE SUITABLE FOR EVERY SITUATION. THIS WORK IS SOLD WITH THE UNDERSTANDING THAT THE PUBLISHER IS NOT ENGAGED IN RENDERING LEGAL, ACCOUNTING, OR OTHER PROFESSIONAL SERVICES. IF PROFESSIONAL ASSISTANCE IS REQUIRED, THE SERVICES OF A COMPETENT PROFESSIONAL PERSON SHOULD BE SOUGHT. NEITHER THE PUBLISHER NOR THE AUTHOR SHALL BE LIABLE FOR DAMAGES ARISING HEREFROM. THE FACT THAT AN ORGANIZATION OR WEBSITE IS REFERRED TO IN THIS WORK AS A CITATION AND/OR A POTENTIAL SOURCE OF FURTHER INFORMATION DOES NOT MEAN THAT THE AUTHOR OR THE PUBLISHER ENDORSES THE INFORMATION THE ORGANIZATION OR WEBSITE MAY PROVIDE OR RECOMMENDATIONS IT MAY MAKE. FURTHER, READERS SHOULD BE AWARE THAT INTERNET WEBSITES LISTED IN THIS WORK MAY HAVE CHANGED OR DISAPPEARED BETWEEN WHEN THIS WORK WAS WRITTEN AND WHEN IT IS READ.

FOR PURPOSES OF ILLUSTRATING THE CONCEPTS AND TECHNIQUES DESCRIBED IN THIS BOOK, THE AUTHOR HAS CREATED VARIOUS NAMES, COMPANY NAMES, MAILING, E-MAIL AND INTERNET ADDRESSES, PHONE AND FAX NUMBERS AND SIMILAR INFORMATION, ALL OF WHICH ARE FICTITIOUS. ANY RESEMBLANCE OF THESE FICTITIOUS NAMES, ADDRESSES, PHONE AND FAX NUMBERS AND SIMILAR INFORMATION TO ANY ACTUAL PERSON, COMPANY AND/OR ORGANIZATION IS UNINTENTIONAL AND PURELY COINCIDENTAL.

WILEY

Wiley Publishing, Inc.

Sales

Contact Wiley
at (800) 762-2974 or
fax (317) 572-4002.

Praise for Visual Books

"Like a lot of other people, I understand things best when I see them visually. Your books really make learning easy and life more fun."

John T. Frey (Cadillac, MI)

"I have quite a few of your Visual books and have been very pleased with all of them. I love the way the lessons are presented!"

Mary Jane Newman (Yorba Linda, CA)

"I just purchased my third Visual book (my first two are dog-eared now!), and, once again, your product has surpassed my expectations.

Tracey Moore (Memphis, TN)

"I am an avid fan of your Visual books. If I need to learn anything, I just buy one of your books and learn the topic in no time. Wonders! I have even trained my friends to give me Visual books as gifts."

Illona Bergstrom (Aventura, FL)

"Thank you for making it so clear. I appreciate it. I will buy many more Visual books."

J.P. Sangdong (North York, Ontario, Canada)

"I have several books from the Visual series and have always found them to be valuable resources."

Stephen P. Miller (Ballston Spa, NY)

"Thank you for the wonderful books you produce. It wasn't until I was an adult that I discovered how I learn — visually. Nothing compares to Visual books. I love the simple layout. I can just grab a book and use it at my computer, lesson by lesson. And I understand the material! You really know the way I think and learn. Thanks so much!"

Stacey Han (Avondale, AZ)

"I absolutely admire your company's work. Your books are terrific. The format is perfect, especially for visual learners like me. Keep them coming!"

Frederick A. Taylor, Jr. (New Port Richey, FL)

"I have several of your Visual books and they are the best I have ever used."

Stanley Clark (Crawfordville, FL)

"I bought my first Teach Yourself VISUALLY book last month. Wow. Now I want to learn everything in this easy format!"

Tom Vial (New York, NY)

"Thank you, thank you, thank you...for making it so easy for me to break into this high-tech world. I now own four of your books. I recommend them to anyone who is a beginner like myself."

Gay O'Donnell (Calgary, Alberta, Canada)

"I write to extend my thanks and appreciation for your books. They are clear, easy to follow, and straight to the point. Keep up the good work! I bought several of your books and they are just right! No regrets! I will always buy your books because they are the best."

Seward Kollie (Dakar, Senegal)

"Compliments to the chef!! Your books are extraordinary! Or, simply put, extra-ordinary, meaning way above the rest! THANKYOU THANKYOU THANKYOU! I buy them for friends, family, and colleagues."

Christine J. Manfrin (Castle Rock, CO)

"What fantastic teaching books you have produced! Congratulations to you and your staff. You deserve the Nobel Prize in Education in the Software category. Thanks for helping me understand computers."

Bruno Tonon (Melbourne, Australia)

"Over time, I have bought a number of your 'Read Less - Learn More' books. For me, they are THE way to learn anything easily. I learn easiest using your method of teaching."

José A. Mazón (Cuba, NY)

"I am an avid purchaser and reader of the Visual series, and they are the greatest computer books I've seen. The Visual books are perfect for people like myself who enjoy the computer, but want to know how to use it more efficiently. Your books have definitely given me a greater understanding of my computer, and have taught me to use it more effectively. Thank you very much for the hard work, effort, and dedication that you put into this series."

Alex Diaz (Las Vegas, NV)

Credits

Project Editor
Maureen Spears

Acquisitions Editor
Jody Lefevere

Product Development Manager
Lindsay Sandman

Copy Editor
Scott Tullis

Technical Editor
Dennis Cohen

Editorial Manager
Robyn Siesky

Manufacturing
Allan Conley
Linda Cook
Paul Gilchrist
Jennifer Guynn

Illustrators
Steven Amory
Matthew Bell
Ronda David-Burroughs
Cheryl Grubbs
Sean Johanessen
Jacob Mansfield
Rita Marley
Tyler Roloff

Book Design
Kathie Rickard

Production Coordinator
Nancee Reeves

Layout
Jennifer Heleine
Amanda Spagnuolo

Screen Artist
Jill A. Proll
Elizabeth Cardenas-Nelson

Proofreader
Laura L. Bowman

Quality Control
Laura Albert

Indexer
Lynnzee Elze

Vice President and Executive Group Publisher
Richard Swadley

Vice President and Publisher
Barry Pruett

Composition Director
Debbie Stailey

About the Authors

Mike Wooldridge is a technology writer, Web developer, and graduate student at UC Berkeley. This is his fourteenth book in the Visual series.

Linda Wooldridge is a former senior editor at *Macworld*. This is her first book.

Authors' Acknowledgments

Mike and **Linda Wooldridge** thank Maureen Spears for her top-notch project editing, Dennis Cohen for his careful technical editing, and Jody Lefevere for assigning them the project. They also thank their five-year-old son for understanding while Mom and Dad spent time writing the book.

TABLE OF CONTENTS

chapter 1   Getting Started

chapter 2   Understanding Photoshop Basics

chapter 3 Changing the Size of an Image

chapter 4 Making Selections

TABLE OF CONTENTS

 **Manipulating Selections**

Painting and Drawing with Color

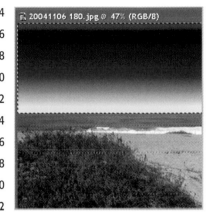

 **chapter 7**   **Adjusting Colors**

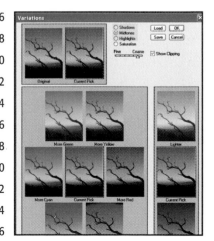

TABLE OF CONTENTS

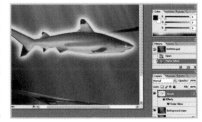

chapter **10** Applying Filters

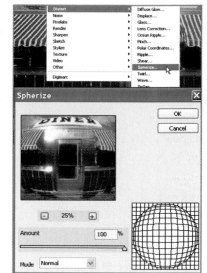

chapter **11** Drawing Shapes

TABLE OF CONTENTS

 **Adding and Manipulating Type**

 **Automating Your Work**

Saving Images

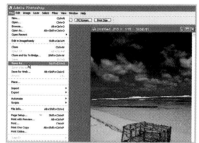

Printing Images

1

Getting Started

Are you interested in creating, modifying, combining, and optimizing digital images on your computer? This chapter introduces you to Adobe Photoshop, a popular software application for working with digital images.

Photoshop enables you to create, modify, combine, and optimize digital images. You can then save the images to print out or use online.

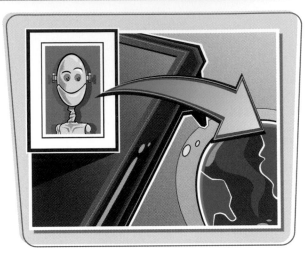

Manipulate Photos

As its name suggests, Photoshop excels at editing digital photographs. You can use the program to make subtle changes, such as adjusting the color in a digital photo or scanned print, or you can use its elaborate filters to make your snapshots look like abstract art. See Chapter 7 for more about adjusting color and Chapter 10 for more about filters.

Paint Pictures

Photoshop's painting features make it a formidable illustration tool as well as a photo editor. You can apply colors or patterns to your images with a variety of brush styles. See Chapter 6 for more about applying color. In addition, you can use the program's typographic tools to integrate stylized letters and words into your images. See Chapter 12 for more about type. You can also create geometric shapes, which are covered in Chapter 11.

Create a Digital Collage

You can combine different image elements in Photoshop. Your compositions can include photos, scanned art, text, and anything else you can save on your computer as a digital image. By placing elements in Photoshop onto separate layers, you can move, transform, and customize them independently of one another. See Chapter 8 for more about layers.

Access and Organize Your Photos

Photoshop's Bridge interface offers an easy-to-use tool to access and preview images that are stored on your computer. See the section "Browse for an Image in Bridge" in this chapter. With Bridge, you can easily tag your images with descriptive information, such as where or when they were taken. You can then use that information to sort your photos. Photoshop also offers useful ways to keep your images organized after you have edited them. You can archive your images on contact sheets or display them in a Web photo gallery. See Chapter 13 for details.

Put Your Images to Work

After you edit your work, you can utilize your images in a variety of ways. Photoshop enables you to print your images, save them in a format suitable for placement on a Web page, or prepare them for use in a page-layout program. See Chapter 15 for more about printing. See Chapter 14 for more about saving images for the Web.

Understanding Photoshop

Photoshop's tools let you move, color, stylize, and add text to your images. You can optimize photographs, or turn them into interesting works of art.

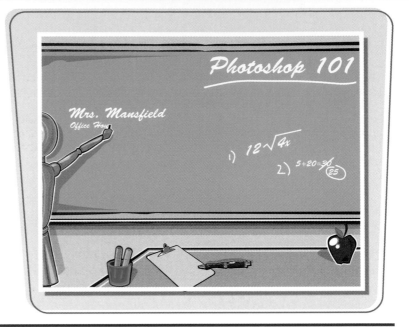

Understanding Pixels

Digital images in Photoshop consist of tiny, solid-color squares called pixels. Photoshop works its magic by rearranging and recoloring these squares. If you zoom in close, you can see the pixels that make up your image. For more about the Zoom tool, see Chapter 2.

Choose Your Pixels

To edit specific pixels in your image, you first must select them by using one of Photoshop's selection tools. You can make geometric selections using the Marquee, or free-form selections using the Lasso tool. See Chapter 4 for more about the selection tools. Photoshop also has a number of commands that help you select specific parts of your image, such as a certain color or range of colors. Other tools enable you to automatically remove objects in your photo from their backgrounds.

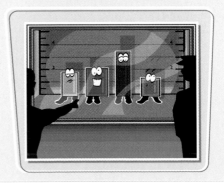

Paint

After selecting your pixels, you can apply color to them by using Photoshop's Paintbrush, Airbrush, and Pencil tools. You can also fill your selections with solid or semitransparent colors, patterns, or pixels copied from another part of your image. Painting is covered in Chapter 6. Special painting tools help you seamlessly cover up objects in your image, or eliminate dust specks or tears from a scanned picture.

Adjust Color

You can brighten, darken, and change the hue of colors in parts of your image with Photoshop's Dodge, Burn, and similar tools. Other commands display interactive dialog boxes that enable you to make wholesale color adjustments, so you can correct overly dark or light digital photographs. See Chapter 7 for details.

Apply Styles and Filters

Photoshop's styles enable you to easily add drop shadows, frame borders, and other effects to your images. You can also perform complex color manipulations or distortions by using filters. Filters can make your image look like an impressionist painting, sharpen or blur your image, or distort your image in various ways. Chapters 9 and 10 cover effects and filters.

Add Type

Photoshop's type tools make it easy to apply titles and labels to your images. You can combine these tools with the program's special effects commands to create warped, 3-D, or wildly colored type. You can find out more about type in Chapter 12.

You can start Photoshop on a PC and begin creating and editing digital images.

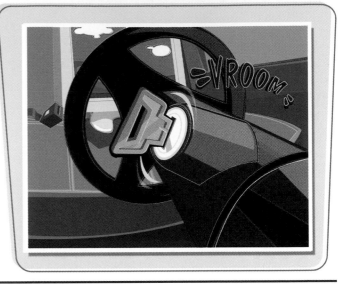

① Click **start**.

② Click **All Programs**.

③ Click **Adobe Photoshop CS2**.

Note: Your path to the Photoshop program may be different, depending on how you installed your software.

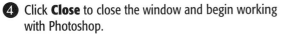

Photoshop starts.

A Welcome Screen window appears.

● You can click a subject to learn more about Photoshop.

④ Click **Close** to close the window and begin working with Photoshop.

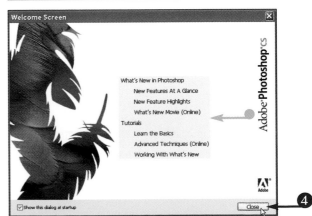

Start Photoshop on a Mac

You can start Photoshop on a Macintosh and begin creating and editing digital images.

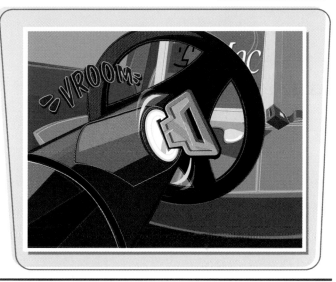

Start Photoshop on a Mac

① Click **Applications**.

② Click the **Adobe Photoshop CS2** folder (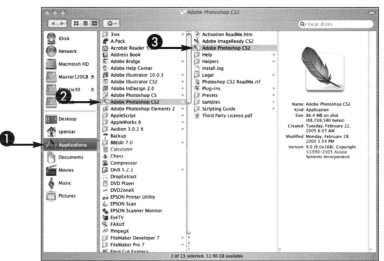).

③ Double-click the **Adobe Photoshop CS2** icon ().

Note: *The exact location of the Adobe Photoshop icon may be different, depending on how you installed your software.*

Photoshop starts.

A Welcome Screen window opens.

● You can click a subject to learn more about Photoshop.

④ Click **Close** to close the window and begin working with Photoshop.

The Photoshop Workspace

You can use a combination of tools, menu commands, and palette-based features to open and edit your digital images in Photoshop.

Menu Bar
Displays the menus that contain most of Photoshop's commands.

Options Bar
Displays controls that let you customize the selected tool in the toolbox.

Palettes
Small, free-floating windows that give you access to common commands and resources.

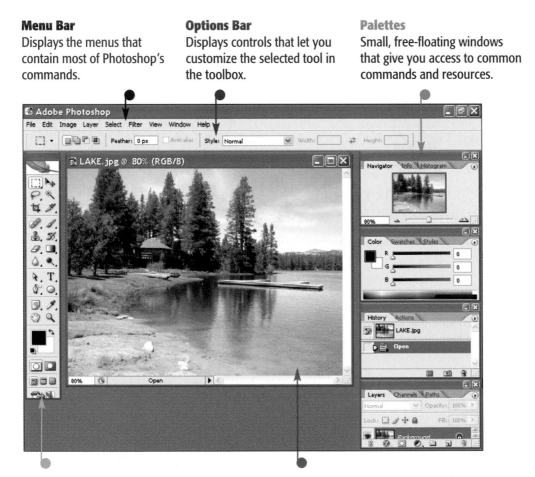

Toolbox
Displays a variety of icons, each one representing an image-editing tool. You click and drag inside your image to apply most of the tools. Also displays the current foreground and background colors.

Image Window
Contains each image you open in Photoshop.

You can get raw material to work with in Photoshop from a variety of sources.

Start from Scratch

You can create your Photoshop image from scratch by opening a blank canvas in the image window. Then you can apply color and patterns with Photoshop's painting tools or cut and paste parts of other images to create a composite. See the section "Create a New Image" in this chapter for more about opening a blank canvas.

Digital Camera Photos

Digital cameras are a great way to transfer digital images onto your computer. Most digital cameras save their images in JPEG or TIFF format, both of which you can open and edit in Photoshop. The program's color adjustment tools are great for correcting color and exposure flaws in digital camera images.

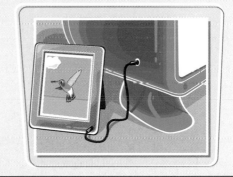

Scanned Photos and Art

A scanner gives you an inexpensive way to convert existing paper-based content into digital form. You can scan photos and art into your computer, retouch and stylize them in Photoshop, and then output them to a color printer.

Stock Photos

A new feature in Photoshop CS2 is the Adobe Stock Photos service. This online service enables you to browse a wide variety of photos — of people, animals, and objects as well as abstract designs — and purchase them for use in image projects. You can access the stock photo service through Adobe Bridge. See the other sections in this chapter for details about Adobe Bridge.

Set Preferences

Photoshop's Preferences dialog boxes enable you to change default settings and customize how the program looks.

Set Preferences

OPEN THE PREFERENCES DIALOG BOX

① Click **Edit** (**Photoshop** on a Mac).

② Click **Preferences**.

③ Click **General**.

The Preferences dialog box appears and displays General options.

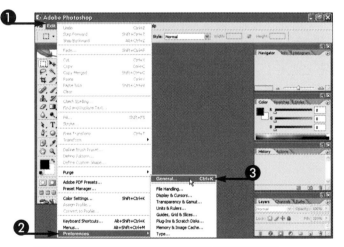

SET GENERAL PREFERENCES

④ Click here to select which dialog box appears when you select a color.

⑤ Type the number of states to store in the History palette.

Note: See Chapter 2 for more about the History palette.

⑥ Click the interface options you want to use (☐ changes to ☑).

⑦ Click here and select **Display & Cursors**.

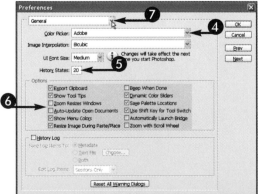

SET DISPLAY AND CURSOR PREFERENCES

The Display & Cursors Preferences options appear.

8 Click a cursor type to use for the painting tools – the Paintbrush, Eraser, and others (○ changes to ⊙).

9 Click a cursor type to use for the other tools (○ changes to ⊙).

10 Click here and select **Units & Rulers**.

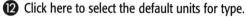

SET UNIT AND RULER PREFERENCES

The Units & Rulers Preferences appear.

11 Click here to select the units for the window rulers.

These units become the default units selected when you resize an image.

12 Click here to select the default units for type.

13 Click **OK**.

Photoshop sets preferences to your specifications.

What type of measurement units should I use in Photoshop?

Typically, you should use the units most applicable to the type of output you intend to use. Pixel units are useful for Web imaging because monitor dimensions are measured in pixels. Inches, centimeters, or picas are useful for print because those are standards for working on paper.

Save a Workspace

You can position the different Photoshop palettes, define keyboard shortcuts, and customize your menus, then save the arrangement as a workspace. This is helpful when several people use Photoshop on the same computer.

Save a Workspace

① Arrange the toolbox and palettes in the Photoshop interface.

② Define any keyboard shortcuts or menus.

● To define keyboard shortcuts and menus, click **Window**, click **Workspace**, and then click **Keyboard Shortcuts & Menus**.

③ Click **Window**.

④ Click **Workspace**.

⑤ Click **Save Workspace**.

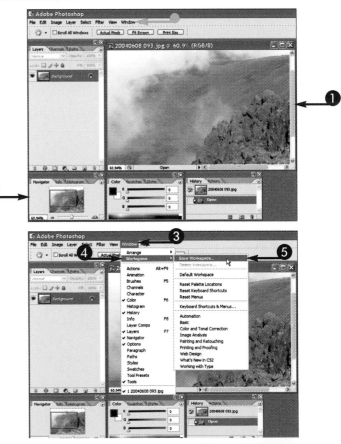

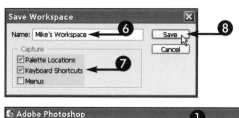

The Save Workspace dialog box appears.

6 Type a name for your workspace.

7 Click the interface elements you want to save (☐ changes to ☑).

8 Click **Save**.

Photoshop saves the workspace.

SELECT A WORKSPACE

1 Click **Window**.

2 Click **Workspace**.

3 Click a workspace.

Photoshop rearranges the workspace.

Photoshop comes with several predefined workspaces.

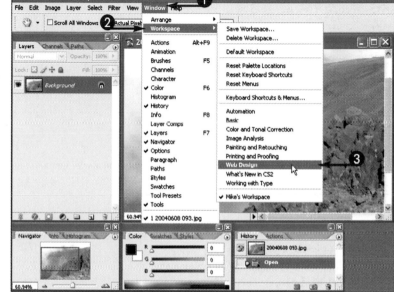

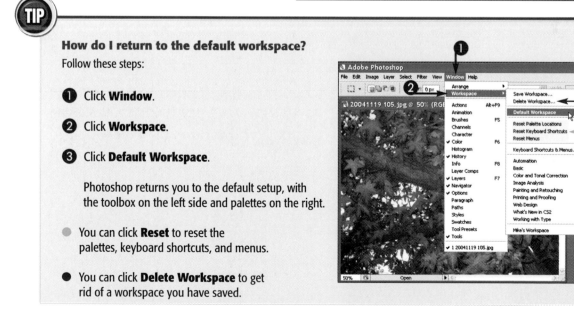

How do I return to the default workspace?

Follow these steps:

1 Click **Window**.

2 Click **Workspace**.

3 Click **Default Workspace**.

Photoshop returns you to the default setup, with the toolbox on the left side and palettes on the right.

● You can click **Reset** to reset the palettes, keyboard shortcuts, and menus.

● You can click **Delete Workspace** to get rid of a workspace you have saved.

Photoshop comes with plenty of electronic documentation that you can access in case you ever need help.

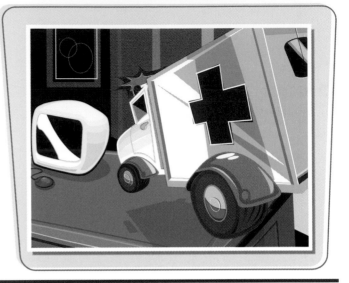

Get Help

① Click **Help**.

② Click **Photoshop Help**.

You can also press F1 (⌘ + /) to access Photoshop Help.

If an Adobe Expert Support dialog box appears, click **Done**.

Photoshop opens the Adobe Help Center window.

You can click a link in the main window pane to explore a general help topic.

③ Click the right arrow buttons (▷) (▷ changes to ▽) to explore a more specific topic.

④ Click the Document icon (▣) to view a topic.

The topic appears in the main window pane.

- You can click the **Previous** and **Next** icons (◀ and ▶) to go to the previous or next topic in the help system.

5 Type a topic in the search box.

6 Click **Search**.

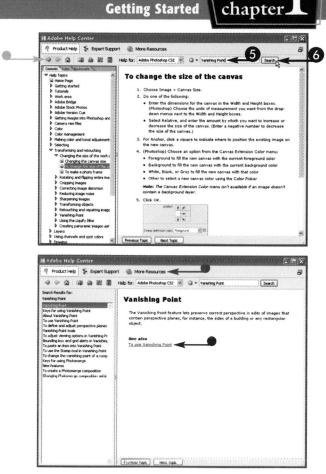

Relevant topics appear in the main window pane.

- You can click a topic to see the information.

- You can click **More Resources** to view links to online help resources.

TIP

How can I use my Photoshop software on another computer?

Photoshop CS2 requires you to activate your software before using it. Activation involves connecting to Adobe via the Internet to confirm that you have a legitimate copy of Photoshop and are not running the software on multiple computers. To move your copy of Photoshop to another computer, you need to transfer the activation by clicking **Help** and then **Transfer Activation** to bring up the Activation Transfer window. Transferring activation will disable the copy of Photoshop on your current computer and allow you to activate a copy of the same software on a different computer.

Open an Image

You can open an existing image file in Photoshop to modify it or use it in a project.

Open an Image

OPEN AN EXISTING IMAGE

① Click **File**.

② Click **Open**.

The Open dialog box appears.

③ Click **Use Adobe Dialog**.

Photoshop switches to a dialog box specific to Adobe applications.

④ Click here to browse to the folder that contains the image you want to open.

⑤ Click the image you want to open.

⑥ Click **Open**.

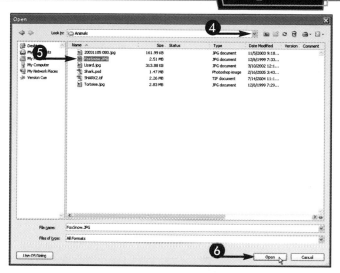

Photoshop opens the image in a new window.

The file name appears in the title bar.

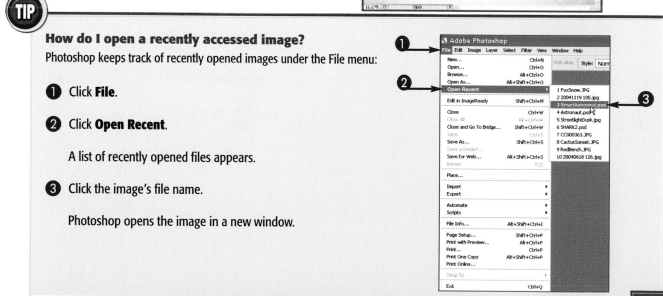

TIP

How do I open a recently accessed image?

Photoshop keeps track of recently opened images under the File menu:

① Click **File**.

② Click **Open Recent**.

A list of recently opened files appears.

③ Click the image's file name.

Photoshop opens the image in a new window.

Browse for an Image in Bridge

You can open an existing image file by using the Adobe Bridge file browser. Bridge offers a user-friendly way to find and open your images.

In Bridge, you can also add descriptive information to your images and sort them. See the sections that follow in this chapter for more information.

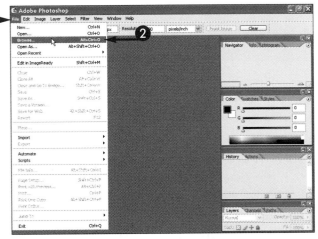

Browse for an Image in Bridge

① Click **File**.

② Click **Browse**.

The Adobe Bridge file browser opens.

③ Click the **Folders** tab.

④ Click the plus button ( ; ▼ on a Mac) to open folders on your computer (in Windows, ⊞ changes to ⊟; on a Mac, ▶ changes to ▼).

⑤ Click a folder on your computer to browse.

The folders and files inside the folder appear.

6 Click an image.

● A preview and information about the image appear.

7 Double-click the image file to open it.

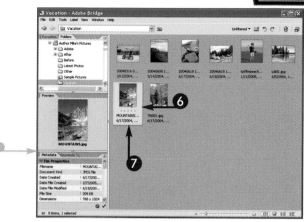

The image opens.

TIPS

How do I add a rating or label to an image in Bridge?

In Bridge, click the image to select it, click **Label**, and then click a star rating or color label. You can apply a rating of from one to five stars, or one of five color labels. Applying ratings or labels to your images enables you to later sort them by rating or label in the Bridge interface. See the section "Sort and Filter Images in Bridge" for more information.

How can I easily access my image folders in Bridge?

You can mark particular folders where you store your images as Favorites in Bridge. To mark a folder as a Favorite, select the folder in the left side of the Bridge window, click **File**, and then click **Add to Favorites**. After you have marked a folder as a Favorite, you can quickly access it by clicking ⌄ at the top of the Bridge interface. A menu appears displaying your Favorite folders as well as recently viewed folders.

You can sort your images by file name, date, file size, dimensions, and other characteristics in Bridge. This can be helpful when you are dealing with hundreds or thousands of images in a collection and need to find a particular image quickly.

You can also filter the information displayed in Bridge, specifying that it only show images with a particular rating or label.

Sort and Filter Images in Bridge

SORT IMAGES

1 Open Adobe Bridge.

2 Click a folder to display its contents.

Note: For details on opening Bridge and selecting folders, see the section "Browse for an Image in Bridge."

3 Click **View**.

4 Click **Sort**.

5 Click a characteristic by which to sort.

Bridge sorts the images.

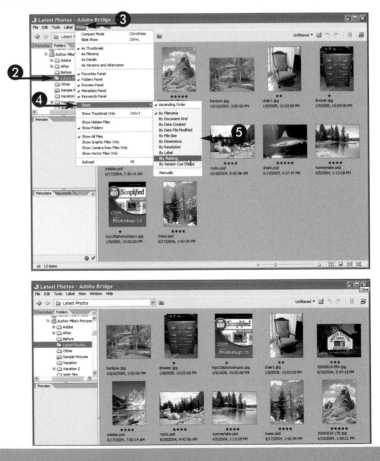

FILTER IMAGES

6 Click **Unfiltered**.

7 Click a rating or label by which to filter your images.

Note: For details about applying ratings and labels, see the section "Browse for an Image in Bridge."

Bridge filters the images, hiding those that are not relevant.

● Unfiltered changes to Filtered.

TIPS

How can I hide folders and nonimage files in Bridge so that only images are displayed?

To hide folders, click **View** and then **Show Folders**. The check mark next to the Show Folders menu item disappears and Bridge hides the folders in the right side of the window. To hide nonimage files as well, click **View** and then **Show Graphic Files Only**.

What image-editing functions can I perform in Bridge?

You can rotate images 90 degrees by clicking the **Rotate 90° counterclockwise** icon (🔄) or the **Rotate 90° clockwise** icon (🔄). You can delete images by selecting them and then clicking the **Trash** icon (🗑). To perform more complex editing, you can return to Photoshop by clicking **File** and then **Return to Adobe Photoshop CS2**.

You can view a set of images in a folder as a slide show in Adobe Bridge. You can control the cycling of the slide show images using keyboard commands.

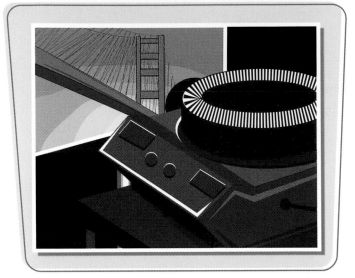

Display a Slide Show in Bridge

1 Open Adobe Bridge.

Note: For more on opening Adobe Bridge, see the section "Sort and Filter Images in Bridge."

2 Click a folder containing the slide show images.

You can also ⌘-click in the main window pane to select the images that you want to display in the slide show.

Note: For details on opening the Bridge and selecting folders, see the section "Browse for an Image in Bridge."

3 Click **View**.

4 Click **Slide Show**.

5 Press .

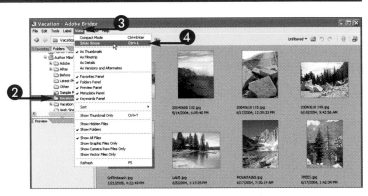

Bridge cycles through the photos in the selected folder.

The order of the photos is determined by the sort order in Bridge.

Note: See the section "Sort and Filter Images in Bridge" for details.

6 Press H.

● Bridge displays the slide show keyboard commands.

7 Press Esc.

The slide show ends.

How can I access stock photos in Bridge?

You can purchase stock photos from Adobe through the Adobe Bridge interface and use those photos in your projects. To access stock photos in Bridge, click the **Favorites** tab and then click **Adobe Stock Photos**. The main Adobe Stock Photos page appears. You can search for stock photos by keyword or browse stock photos by category. The service allows you to download low-resolution "comp" versions of photos to try out free for 30 days.

How am I allowed to use stock photos purchased from Adobe?

Images that you purchase through Adobe's stock photo service may be used on a "royalty-free" basis. This means you pay a single licensing fee, which varies based on the resolution of the image. The royalty-free license grants you the right to use that image multiple times in a variety of ways, including for advertising, on product merchandise, and on Web sites. For details, see the license agreement on the stock photo pages.

You can start a Photoshop project by creating a blank image.

Create a New Image

① Click **File**.

② Click **New**.

The New dialog box appears.

③ Type a name for the new image.

● You can click here to select a preset image size.

④ Type the dimensions and resolution you want.

⑤ Click **OK**.

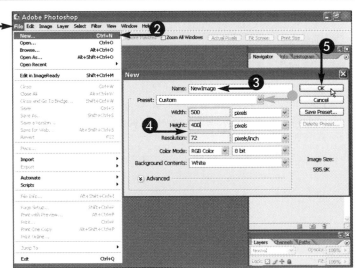

Photoshop creates a new image window at the specified dimensions.

● The file name appears in the title bar.

⑥ Use Photoshop's tools and commands to create your image.

Note: See the following chapters for more on using the Photoshop tools and commands. To save your image, see Chapter 14.

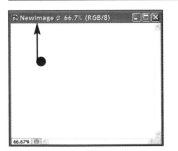

You can exit Photoshop after
you finish using the application.

Exit Photoshop

EXIT PHOTOSHOP ON A PC

① Click **File**.

② Click **Exit**.

Photoshop exits.

Before exiting, Photoshop alerts you to any open
images that have unsaved changes so you can
save them.

Note: See Chapter 14 to save image files.

EXIT PHOTOSHOP ON A MAC

① Click **Photoshop**.

② Click **Quit Photoshop**.

Photoshop exits.

Before exiting, Photoshop alerts you to any open
images that have unsaved changes so you can
save them.

Note: See Chapter 14 to save image files.

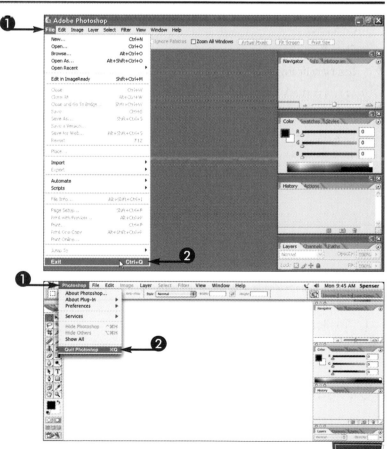

CHAPTER 2

Understanding Photoshop Basics

Are you ready to start working with images? This chapter shows you how to select tools and fine-tune your workspace.

Magnify with the Zoom Tool

You can change the magnification of an image with the Zoom tool. With this tool, you can view small details in an image or view an image at full size.

Magnify with the Zoom Tool

INCREASE MAGNIFICATION

1 Click the **Zoom** tool ( ).

 changes to .

2 Click the image.

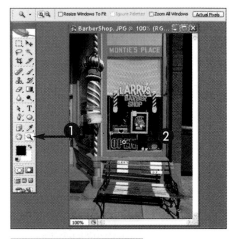

Photoshop increases the magnification of the image.

The point that you clicked in the image is centered in the window.

● The current magnification shows in the title bar and status bar.

You can choose an exact magnification by typing a percentage value in the status bar.

DECREASE MAGNIFICATION

1 Click the **Zoom Out** icon (🔍).

   ⬧ changes to 🔍.

2 Click the image.

   Photoshop decreases the magnification of the image.

● The current magnification shows in the title bar and status bar.

   You can also press and hold **Alt** (**Option** on the Mac) and click the image to decrease magnification.

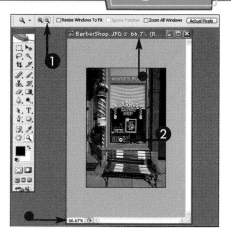

MAGNIFY A DETAIL

1 Click the **Zoom In** icon (🔍).

2 Click and drag with 🔍 to select the detail.

   The image appears enlarged on-screen.

TIP

How do I quickly return an image to 100% magnification?

You have three different ways to return the image to 100% magnification:

1 By double-clicking the **Zoom** tool (🔍).

2 By clicking **Actual Pixels** on the Options bar.

3 By clicking **View** and then **Actual Pixels** from the menu.

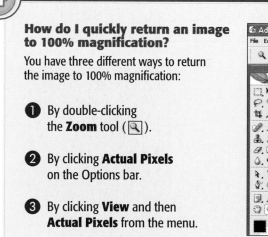
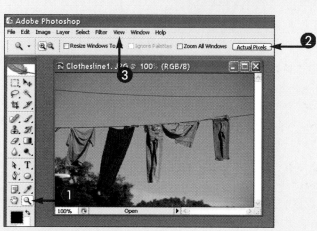

You can move an image within the window by using the Hand tool or scroll bars. The Hand tool helps you navigate to an exact area on the image.

The Hand tool is a more flexible alternative to using the scroll bars because, unlike the scroll bars, the Hand tool enables you to drag the image freely in two dimensions.

USING THE HAND TOOL

① Click the **Hand** tool (⊞).

Note: For ⊞ to produce an effect, the image must extend outside the boundary of the image window.

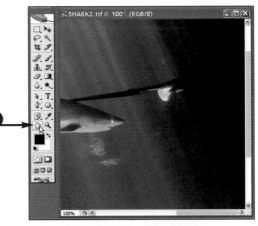

⇧ changes to a hand pointer (⊞).

② Click and drag ⊞ inside the image window.

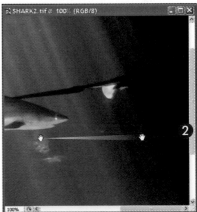

The view of the image shifts inside the window.

● The Navigator palette displays the view relative to the entire image.

USING THE SCROLL BARS

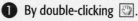

1 Click and hold one of the window's scroll bar buttons.

The image scrolls.

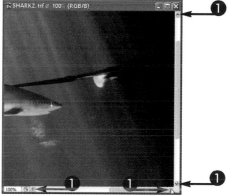

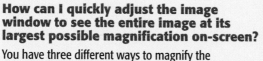

TIP

How can I quickly adjust the image window to see the entire image at its largest possible magnification on-screen?

You have three different ways to magnify the image to its largest possible size:

1 By double-clicking 🖐.

2 By clicking **Fit Screen** on the Options bar.

3 By clicking **View** and then **Fit on Screen** from the menu.

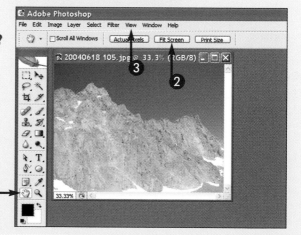

Change Screen Modes

You can switch the screen mode to change the look of your workspace on-screen.

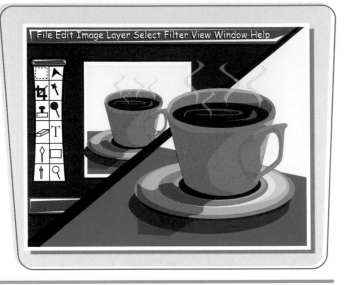

In the standard screen mode, you can view multiple images at the same time, each in a different window.

SWITCH TO FULL SCREEN MODE WITH MENU BAR

1 Click the **Full Screen Mode with Menu Bar** tool (▣).

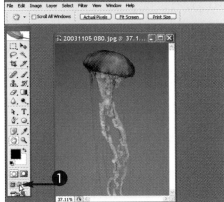

Photoshop places the current image window in the center of a blank, full screen canvas with the menu bar at the top of the screen.

The status bar is not visible when you click ▣.

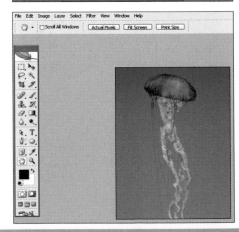

SWITCH TO FULL SCREEN

1 Click the **Full Screen Mode** tool (▣).

The image appears full screen without the menu bar, but with the Options bar, toolbox, and palettes still present.

The status bar is not visible in full screen mode.

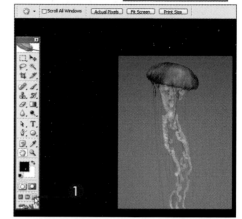

CLOSE TOOLBOX AND PALETTES

1 Press Tab .

Photoshop closes all toolboxes and palettes.

Note: Pressing Tab closes all toolboxes and palettes in all of Photoshop's screen modes.

Note: To view the toolbox and palettes, you can press Tab again.

TIPS

How do I display the menu bar when in full screen mode?

Press Shift + F to toggle the view of the menu bar in full screen mode.

Are there shortcuts for selecting tools from the toolbox?

You can press letter keys to quickly select items in the toolbox. You may find this more efficient than clicking tools. To view the letter for a tool, move your cursor (↖) over the tool until a yellow tip box appears. Here are the shortcut letters for the more popular tools:

Tool Name	Shortcut	Tool Name	Shortcut
Marquee	M	Type	T
Move	V	Zoom	Z
Lasso	L	Eraser	E
Paintbrush	B	Magic Wand	W

You can turn on rulers and position guides to help place elements accurately in your image.

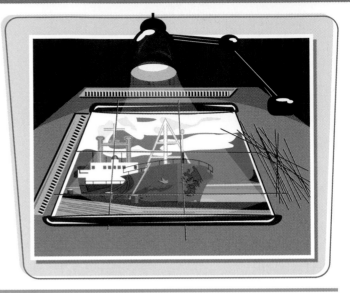

Guides help you position the different elements that make up your Photoshop image with more precision. These lines do not appear on the printed image.

View Rulers and Guides

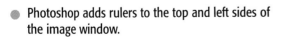

1 Click **View**.

2 Click **Rulers**.

Note: *To change the rulers' units of measurement and other preferences, see Chapter 1.*

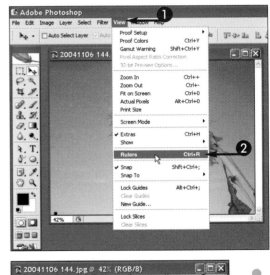

● Photoshop adds rulers to the top and left sides of the image window.

3 Click one of the rulers and drag the cursor into the window (⌂ changes to ⊕).

Drag the top ruler down to create a horizontal guide.

Drag the left ruler to the right to create a vertical guide.

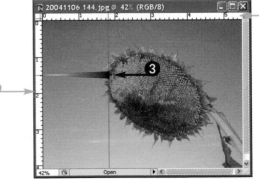

● A thin, colored line called a guide appears.

● You can also click **View** and then **New Guide** to add a guide.

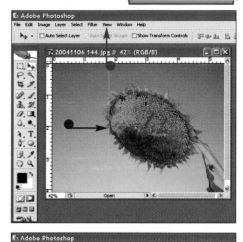

MOVE A GUIDE

1 Click the **Move** tool (⊕).

    changes to ╫.

2 Position ╫ over a guide and click and drag.

The guide adjusts to its new placement.

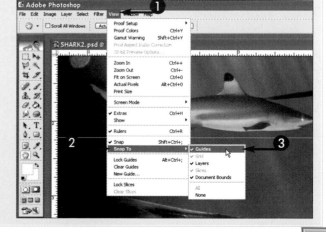

How do I make objects in my images "snap to" my guides when I move those objects?

The "snap to" feature is useful for aligning elements in a row horizontally or in a column vertically. To make objects in the different layers of your image automatically snap to any nearby guides:

1 Click **View**.

2 Click **Snap To**.

3 Click **Guides**.

When you move an object, Photoshop automatically "snaps" it to the nearest guide.

Note: For more about layers, see Chapter 8.

You can undo multiple commands using the History palette. This enables you to correct mistakes or change your mind about elements of your image.

The History palette lists recently executed commands with the most recent command at the bottom.

Undo Commands

1. Click **Window**.
2. Click **History**.
3. Click and drag the History slider (◻) upward.

● Alternatively, you can click a previous command in the History palette.

● Photoshop undoes the previous commands.

You can click and drag the slider down to redo the commands.

Revert an Image

You can revert an image to the previously saved state and start your image editing again.

Revert an Image

1 Click **File**.

2 Click **Revert**.

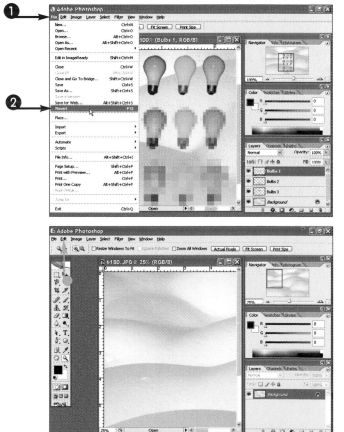

Photoshop reverts the image to its previously saved state.

● You can click **Edit** and then **Undo Revert** to return to the unreverted state.

CHAPTER

3

Changing the Size of an Image

Do you want to change the size of your image? This chapter shows you how to change an image's on-screen size, print size, and print resolution, as well as how to crop an image.

Change the On-Screen Size of an Image

You can change the size at which an image displays on your computer monitor so that users can see the entire image.

Because you lose less sharpness when you decrease an image's size than when you increase it, consider starting with an image that is too big rather than one that is too small.

Change the On-Screen Size of an Image

① Click **Image**.

② Click **Image Size**.

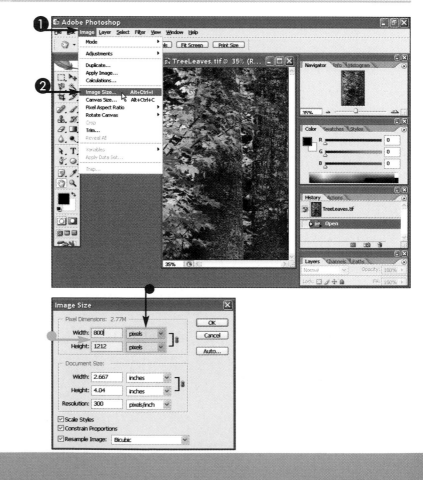

● The Image Size dialog box appears, listing the on-screen height and width of the image.

● To resize by a certain percentage, you can click here and change the units to percent.

3 Type a size for a dimension.

● You can click **Constrain Proportions**
(☐ changes to ☑) to force the other
dimension to change proportionally.

4 Click **OK**.

● You can restore the original dialog box settings
by holding down Alt (Option on a Mac) and
clicking **Cancel**, which changes to **Reset**.

Photoshop resizes the image.

Note: *Changing the number of pixels in an image can add blur. To sharpen
a resized image, apply the Unsharp Mask filter as covered in Chapter 10.*

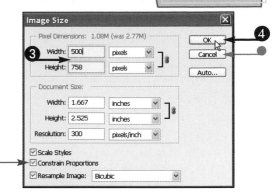

TIPS

**What is the difference between
an image's on-screen size and its
print size?**

On-screen size depends only on the
number of pixels that
make up an image.
Print size depends on
the number of pixels
as well as on the print
resolution, which is
the density of the pixels
on a printed page.
Higher resolutions print a
smaller image, and lower
resolutions print a larger
image, given the same
on-screen size.

**What size should I make my image so
that it takes up the area of a Web
browser window?**

The majority of users set their monitors to
resolutions of at least 800 pixels wide by
600 pixels tall. As a result, most Web
browser windows, when
maximized, can accommodate
images that are approximately
750 pixels or smaller in width.
It is harder to estimate height,
because the maximum size
available depends on the
toolbar settings in your browser.
Images that are 350 pixels high
will fit inside most browser
windows.

Change the Print Size of an Image

You can change the printed size of an image to determine how it appears on paper.

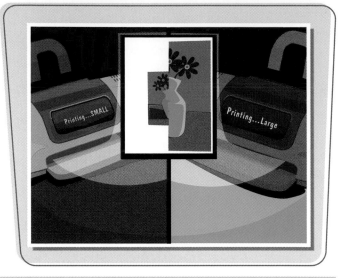

① Click **Image**.

② Click **Image Size**.

● The Image Size dialog box appears, listing the current height and width of the printed image.

● You can click here to change the unit of measurement.

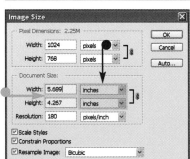

③ Type a size for a dimension.

● You can click **Constrain Proportions** (☐ changes to ☑) to force the other dimension to change proportionally.

④ Click **OK**.

● You can restore the original dialog box settings by holding down Alt (Option on a Mac) and clicking **Cancel**, which changes to **Reset**.

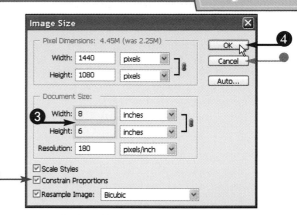

Photoshop resizes the image.

Note: *Changing the number of pixels in an image can add blur. To sharpen a resized image, apply the Unsharp Mask filter as covered in Chapter 10.*

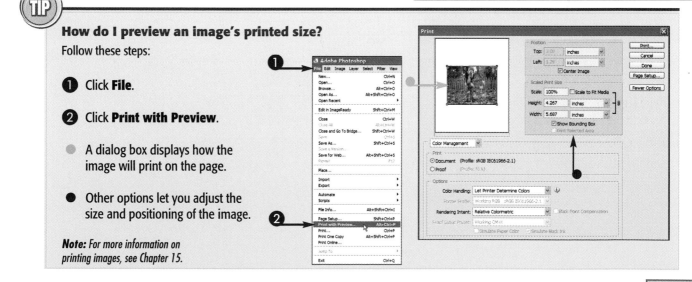

TIP

How do I preview an image's printed size?
Follow these steps:

① Click **File**.

② Click **Print with Preview**.

● A dialog box displays how the image will print on the page.

● Other options let you adjust the size and positioning of the image.

Note: *For more information on printing images, see Chapter 15.*

Change the Resolution of an Image

You can change the print resolution of an image to increase or decrease the print quality.

The resolution, combined with the number of pixels in an image, determines the size of a printed image.

The greater the resolution, the better the image looks on the printed page – up to a limit, which varies with the type of printer and paper quality.

Change the Resolution of an Image

① Click **Image**.

② Click **Image Size**.

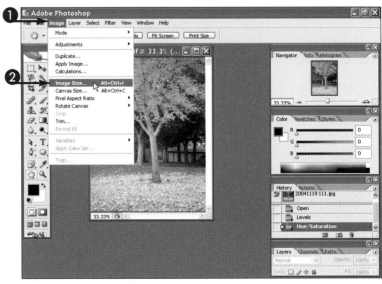

● The Image Size dialog box appears, listing the current resolution of the image.

● You can click here to change the resolution units.

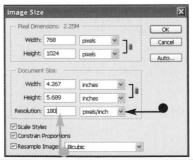

3 Type a new resolution.

● You can click **Resample Image**
(☐ changes to ☑) to adjust the number
of pixels in your image and keep the print
dimensions fixed.

4 Click **OK**.

● You can restore the original dialog box settings
by holding down `Alt` (`Option` on a Mac) and
clicking **Cancel**, which changes to **Reset**.

If you clicked **Resample Image**, the change in
resolution changes the number of pixels in the
image. The on-screen image changes in size
while the print size stays the same.

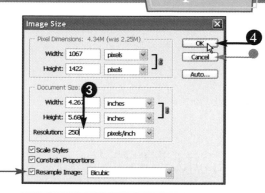

TIPS

What is the relationship between resolution, on-screen size, and print size?

To determine the printed size of a Photoshop image, you can divide the on-screen size by the resolution. If you have an image with an on-screen width of 480 pixels and a resolution of 120 pixels per inch, the printed width is 4 inches.

How can I use the Measure ( ) tool to measure dimensions in my image?

Click and hold the **Eyedropper** tool ( ) and click the **Measure** tool ( ). With you can click and drag inside your image to measure dimensions of objects. Click **Window** and then **Info** to open the Info palette to see your measurements. You can change the Info palette units in the Units & Rulers preferences. See Chapter 1 for details about changing preferences.

Crop an Image

You can use the Crop tool to change the size of an image to remove unneeded space on the top, bottom, and sides.

CROP ONLY

① Click the **Crop** tool (⬚).

  ⬚ changes to ⬚.

② Click and drag ⬚ to select the area of the image you want to keep.

  You can also crop an image by changing its canvas size.

Note: See the section "Change the Canvas Size of an Image" for more information.

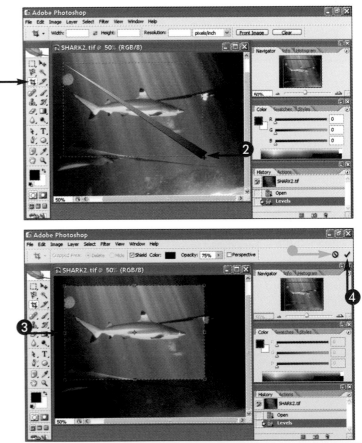

③ Click and drag the side and corner handles (☐) to adjust the size of the cropping boundary.

  You can click and drag inside the cropping boundary to move it without adjusting its size.

④ Click the check mark (✓) or press Enter (Return on a Mac).

● To exit the cropping process, you can press Esc (Esc or ⌘+. on a Mac) or click the **Cancel** icon (⊘).

Photoshop crops the image, deleting the pixels outside of the cropping boundary.

ROTATE AND CROP

1 Perform steps **1** to **3** on the previous page.

2 Click and drag outside of the boundary lines.

3 Click ✓ or press **Enter** (**Return** on a Mac).

Photoshop rotates the image and crops it.

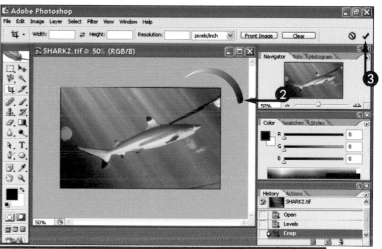

TIP

How can I constrain the proportions of the Crop tool?

Perform the following steps:

1 Type the width and height of the cropping boundary in the Options bar.

● You can also specify a final resolution in the Options bar.

2 Drag 🔲 to apply the Crop tool.

Photoshop constrains the rectangle to the specified dimensions.

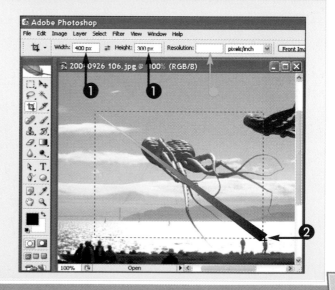

Crop and Straighten Photos

You can automatically crop and straighten one or more photographs in a Photoshop image. After cropping and straightening, Photoshop places each image in its own image window. This feature is useful if you have digitized several images at the same time on a scanner and want to separate them.

Crop and Straighten Photos

① Click **File**.

② Click **Automate**.

③ Click **Crop and Straighten Photos**.

● Photoshop straightens the photos, crops out any blank space, and copies the photos to separate image windows.

Note: To save the newly cropped images, see Chapter 14.

● The original image remains in its own window.

Trim an Image

You can use the Trim command to automatically remove any blank space surrounding your image. This can be useful for scanned photos, or when you want to minimize the file size of an image.

Trim an Image

1 Click **Image**.

2 Click **Trim**.

The Trim dialog box appears.

3 Click the type of pixels you want to trim away (○ changes to ⦿).

4 Click the areas to trim away (☐ changes to ☑).

5 Click **OK**.

Photoshop trims the image.

Change the Canvas Size of an Image

You can alter the canvas size of an image in order to change its aspect ratio or to add blank space around its borders.

The *canvas* is the area on which an image sits. Changing the canvas size is one way to crop an image.

The Crop tool provides an alternative to changing the canvas size. See the section "Crop an Image" for more information.

Change the Canvas Size of an Image

① Click **Image**.

② Click **Canvas Size**.

● The Canvas Size dialog box appears, listing the current dimensions of the canvas.

● You can click here to change the unit of measurement.

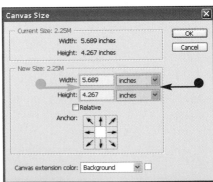

③ Type the new canvas dimensions.

● You can modify in what directions Photoshop changes the canvas size by clicking an anchor point.

● You can specify the color with which Photoshop will fill any new canvas area if you enlarge a dimension.

④ Click **OK**.

Note: *If you decrease a dimension, Photoshop displays a dialog box asking whether you want to proceed. Click* ***Proceed***.

Photoshop changes the image's canvas size.

Because the middle anchor point is selected in this example, the canvas size changes equally on opposite sides.

TIPS

How do I increase the area of an image using the Crop tool?

You can enlarge the image window by clicking and dragging the lower right-hand corner of the window to add extra space around the image. Then, you can apply the Crop tool so that the cropping boundary extends beyond the borders of the image. When you apply cropping, the image canvas enlarges. Photoshop applies the current background color in the new space. For more about selecting colors, see Chapter 6.

How can I crop without making the image canvas smaller?

Use a lasso tool, such as, the **Rectangular Marquee** (▢) tool, to select a cropping boundary. Cick **Select** and then **Inverse** to select the area outside the boundary. Pressing `Backspace` (`Delete` on a Mac) crops the image, but keeps your canvas dimensions the same. If you are working with a multilayer image, this technique only crops content in the selected layer.

4

Making Selections

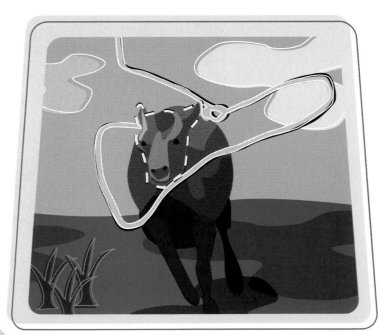

Do you want to move, color, or transform parts of your image independently of the rest of the image? The first step is to make a selection. This chapter shows you how.

Select with the Marquee Tools

You can select a rectangular or elliptical area of your image by using the Marquee tools. Then you can move, delete, or stylize the selected area using other Photoshop commands.

USING THE RECTANGULAR MARQUEE TOOL

① Click the **Rectangular Marquee** tool (▢).

    ⬚ changes to +.

② Click and drag diagonally inside the image window.

    You can hold down **Shift** while you click and drag to create a square selection.

- Photoshop selects a rectangular portion of your image. You can now perform other commands on the selection.

- You can deselect a selection by clicking **Select** and then **Deselect**.

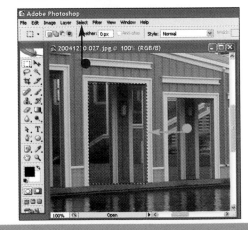

USING THE ELLIPTICAL MARQUEE TOOL

① Click and hold the ⬚.

② From the list that appears, click **Elliptical Marquee Tool** (⬭).

    ↳ changes to ✛.

③ Click and drag diagonally inside the image window.

You can hold down **Shift** while you click and drag to create a circular selection.

● Photoshop selects an elliptical portion of your image.

You can now perform other commands on the selection.

● You can deselect a selection by clicking **Select** and then **Deselect**.

TIP

How do I customize the Marquee tools?

You can customize the Marquee tools (⬚ and ⬭) by using the text fields and menus in the Options bar.

Feather: Typing a **Feather** value softens your selection edge — which means that Photoshop partially selects pixels near the edge.

Style: You can click the **Style** ⌄ (▣) to define your Marquee tool as a fixed size or fixed aspect ratio.

Height and Width: You can specify the fixed dimensions in the **Width** and **Height** boxes.

Select with the Lasso Tool

You can create irregular selections with the Lasso tools. Then you can move, delete, or stylize the selected area using other Photoshop commands.

You can use the regular Lasso tool to create curved or jagged selections. With the Polygonal Lasso tool, you can easily create a selection made up of many straight lines.

Select with the Lasso Tool

USING THE REGULAR LASSO

① Click the **Lasso** tool (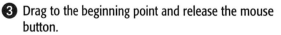).

② Click and drag your cursor ( ) to make a selection.

● To accurately trace a complicated edge, you can magnify that part of the image with the **Zoom** tool ( ).

Note: See Chapter 2 for more about the Zoom tool.

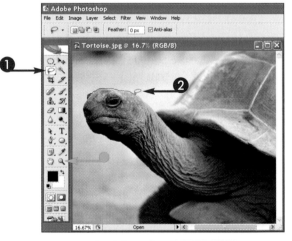

③ Drag to the beginning point and release the mouse button.

The selection is now complete.

USING THE POLYGONAL LASSO

① Click and hold ⌞P⌟.

② From the list that appears, click **Polygonal Lasso Tool** (⌞P⌟).

   ⌖ changes to ⌖.

③ Click multiple times along the border of the area you want to select.

④ To complete the selection, click the starting point.

You can also double-click anywhere in the image and Photoshop adds a final straight line connected to the starting point.

The selection is now complete.

You can achieve a polygonal effect with the regular Lasso tool by pressing Alt (Option on the Mac) and clicking to make your selection.

TIP

What if my lasso selection is not as precise as I want it to be?

Selecting complicated outlines with the ⌞P⌟ can be difficult, even for the steadiest of hands. To fix an imprecise Lasso selection, you can

- Deselect the selection, by clicking **Select** and then **Deselect**, and try again.

- Try to fix your selection. See the section "Add to or Subtract from Your Selection."

- Switch to the **Magnetic Lasso** tool (⌞P⌟). See the section "Select with the Magnetic Lasso Tool."

Select with the Magnetic Lasso Tool

You can select elements of your image that have well-defined edges quickly and easily with the Magnetic Lasso tool.

The Magnetic Lasso works best when the element you are trying to select contrasts sharply with its background.

Select with the Magnetic Lasso Tool

① Click and hold ▱.

② Click **Magnetic Lasso Tool** (▱) from the list that appears.

③ Click the edge of the object you want to select.

This creates a beginning anchor point.

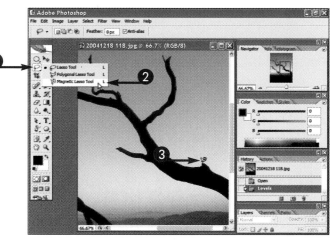

④ Drag your Magnetic Lasso cursor (▱) along the edge of the object.

The Magnetic Lasso's path snaps to the edge of the element as you drag.

● To help guide the lasso, you can click to add anchor points as you go along the path.

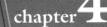

5 Click the beginning anchor point to finish your selection.

Alternatively, you can double-click anywhere in the image and Photoshop completes the selection for you.

The path is complete.

This example shows that the Magnetic Lasso is less useful for selecting areas where you find little contrast between the image and its background.

 TIP

How can I adjust the precision of the Magnetic Lasso tool?

You can use the Options bar to adjust the Magnetic Lasso tool's precision:

Width: The number of nearby pixels the lasso considers when creating a selection. If you magnify the edge you are selecting, you can typically decrease the width.

Edge Contrast: How much contrast is required for the lasso to consider something an edge. You can decrease the edge contrast to select fuzzier edges.

Frequency: The frequency of the anchor points. You can increase the frequency for better precision when selecting poorly defined edges.

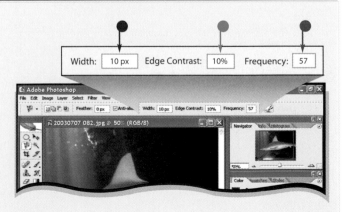

Select with the Magic Wand Tool

You can select groups of similarly colored pixels with the Magic Wand tool. You may find this useful if you want to remove an object from a background.

You can control how precisely the tool makes the selection by choosing a tolerance value from 0 to 255.

Select with the Magic Wand Tool

① Click the **Magic Wand** tool (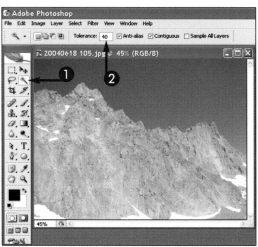).

② Type a number from 0 to 255 in the Tolerance field.

To select a narrow range of colors, type a small number; to select a wide range of colors, type a large number.

③ Click the cursor (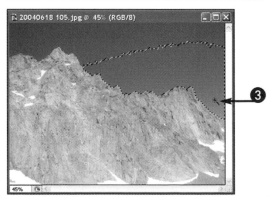) in the area you want to select inside the image.

Photoshop selects the pixel you clicked, plus any similarly colored pixels near it.

④ To add to your selection, press **Shift** and click elsewhere in the image.

● You can also click the **Add to Selection** button () in the Options bar.

Photoshop adds to your selection.

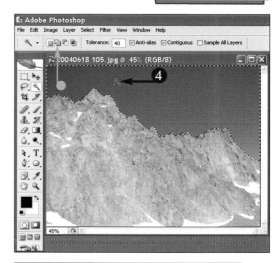

⑤ To delete the selected pixels, press **Backspace** (**Delete** on a Mac).

Photoshop replaces the pixels with the background color.

In this example, Photoshop replaces the pixels with white.

If you make the selection in a layer, the deleted selection becomes transparent.

Note: *See Chapter 8 for more about layers.*

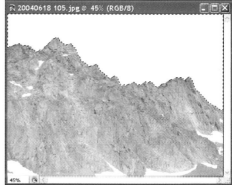

TIP

How can I help ensure that the Magic Wand tool selects all the instances of a color in an image?

You can deselect **Contiguous** (☑ changes to ☐) in the Options bar so that the Magic Wand tool selects similar colors, even when they are not contiguous with the pixel you click with the tool. This can be useful when objects intersect the solid-color areas of your image. You can also select **Sample All Layers** (☑ changes to ☑) to select similar colors in all layers in the image, not just the currently selected layer.

Select with the Color Range Command

You can select a set range of colors within an image with the Color Range command. With this command, you can quickly select a region of relatively solid color, such as a sky or a blank wall.

① Click **Select**.

② Click **Color Range**.

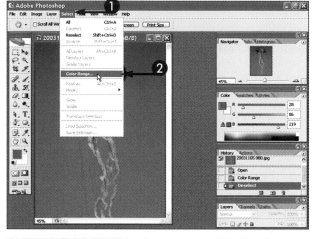

The Color Range dialog box appears.

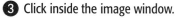 changes to ⬚.

③ Click inside the image window.

● Photoshop selects all the pixels in the image that are similar to the pixel you clicked. These areas turn white in the Color Range window.

● The number of pixels that turn white depends on the Fuzziness setting.

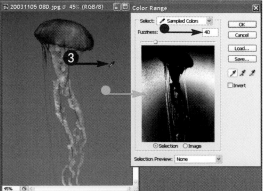

④ To increase the range of color, click and drag the Fuzziness slider (⬜) to the right.

You can decrease the color range by dragging the slider to the left.

● You can also broaden the selected area by clicking the **Add Eyedropper** icon (📷) and then clicking other parts of the image.

⑤ Click **OK**.

Photoshop makes the selection in the main image window.

Note: *Sometimes the Color Range command selects unwanted areas of the image. To eliminate these areas, see the section "Add to or Subtract from Your Selection."*

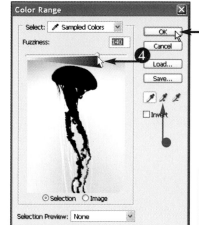

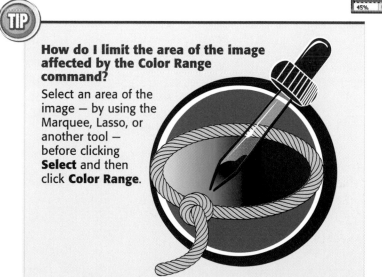

TIP

How do I limit the area of the image affected by the Color Range command?

Select an area of the image — by using the Marquee, Lasso, or another tool — before clicking **Select** and then click **Color Range**.

Select All the Pixels in an Image

You can select all the pixels in an image by using a single command. This lets you perform a different command on the entire image, such as copying it to a different image window.

With the entire image window selected, you can easily delete your image, or copy and paste it into another window. For multilayer images, this technique selects all the pixels in the current layer.

Select All the Pixels in an Image

① Click **Select**.

② Click **All**.

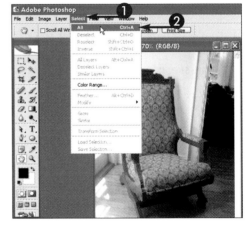

You can also press `Ctrl` + `A` (`⌘` + `A` on the Mac) to select all the pixels in an image.

● Photoshop selects the entire image window.

You can delete your image by pressing `Delete`.

To copy your image, press `Ctrl` + `C` (`⌘` + `C` on the Mac).

To paste your image, press `Ctrl` + `V` (`⌘` + `V` on the Mac).

Move a Selection Border

You can move a selection border if your original selection is not in the intended place.

Move a Selection Border

① Select , ▭, ◯, or ✎.

Note: For more about the various selection tools, see the previous sections in this chapter.

● Make sure you click the **New Selection** button ▦.

② Make a selection with the selection tool.

③ Click and drag inside the selection.

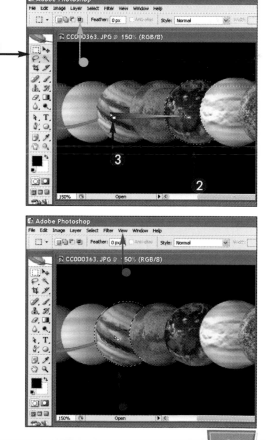

● The selection border moves.

To move your selection one pixel at a time, you can use the arrow keys on your keyboard.

● You can hide a selection by clicking **View** and then **Selection Edges**.

Add to or Subtract from Your Selection

You can add to or subtract from your selection by using various selection tools.

Add to or Subtract from Your Selection

ADD TO A SELECTION

① Make a selection using one of Photoshop's selection tools (▢, ♀, or ✦).

② Click a selection tool.

This example illustrates the use of the ♀.

Note: See the previous sections in this chapter to select the appropriate tool for your image.

③ Click ▣.

④ Select the area you want to add.

⑤ Complete the selection by closing the path.

● The original selection enlarges.

You can enlarge the selection further by repeating steps **2** to **5**.

You can also add to a selection by pressing Shift as you make your selection.

SUBTRACT FROM A SELECTION

① Make a selection using one of Photoshop's selection tools.

② Click a selection tool.

This example illustrates the use of the 🔲.

③ Click the **Subtract from Selection** button (🔲).

④ Select the area you want to subtract.

● Photoshop deselects, or subtracts, the selected area.

You can subtract other parts of the selection by repeating steps **2** to **4**.

You can also subtract from a selection by holding down **Alt** (**Option** on the Mac) as you make your selection.

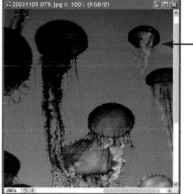

TIPS

What tools can I use to add to or subtract from a selection?

You can use any of the Marquee, Lasso, or Magic Wand tools (🔲, 🔎, or 🪄), discussed in previous sections in this chapter, to add to or subtract from a selection. All three have Add to Selection and Subtract from Selection buttons available in the Options bar when you select them.

How can I expand or contract a selection?

To expand a selection, click **Select**, **Modify**, and then **Expand**. A dialog box appears, enabling you to specify the amount of expansion in pixels. To contract a selection, click **Select**, **Modify**, and then **Contract**. A dialog box appears, enabling you to specify the amount of contraction in pixels.

Invert a Selection

You can invert a selection to deselect what is currently selected and select everything else. This is useful when you want to select the background around an object.

① Make a selection using one of Photoshop's selection tools.

Note: For more about the various selection tools, see the previous sections in this chapter.

② Click **Select**.

③ Click **Inverse**.

Photoshop inverts the selection.

Grow a Selection

You can increase the size of your selection using the Grow command, which is useful when you want to include similarly colored, neighboring pixels in your selection.

Grow a Selection

1 Make a selection using one of Photoshop's selection tools.

Note: To learn more about the various selection tools, see the previous sections in this chapter.

2 Click **Select**.

3 Click **Grow**.

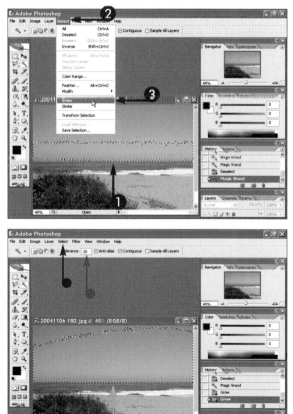

● The selection grows to include similarly colored pixels contiguous with the current selection.

● To include noncontiguous pixels as well, you can click **Select** and then **Similar**.

● You can change the number of similarly colored pixels the Grow command selects by changing the Tolerance setting; click 🔍, type a new number in the Tolerance field, make your selection, and click **Select** and then **Grow**.

You can divide a large image that you want to display on the Web into smaller rectangular sections called *slices*. The different slices of an image can then be optimized independently of one another for faster download. See Chapter 14 for details.

You can also use slices to create special Web effects, such as rollovers, in ImageReady. ImageReady is a Web imaging program that comes with Photoshop.

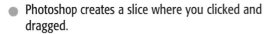

Create Slices

① Click the **Slice** tool (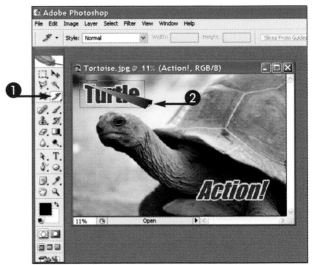).

  changes to ✐.

② Click and drag inside the image to create a slice.

● Photoshop creates a slice where you clicked and dragged.

Note: Slices you define are called user-slices.

  Photoshop fills in the rest of the image with auto-slices.

Note: User-slices remain fixed when you add more slices to your image, whereas auto-slices can change size.

③ Click and drag to define another slice in your image.

● Photoshop creates another slice where you clicked and dragged.

Photoshop creates or rearranges auto-slices to fill in the rest of the image.

Note: To save the different slices for the Web, see Chapter 14. For more about how to use slices in ImageReady, see Photoshop's Help information. See Chapter 1 to access Photoshop Help.

TIP

How do I resize or delete slices in my image?

First, select the Slice Select tool (🔲), which is accessible by clicking and holding 🔲. To resize a user-slice, click inside it and then click and drag a border handle. To delete a user-slice, click inside it and then press `Backspace` (`Delete` on a Mac). When you resize or delete slices, Photoshop automatically resizes auto-slices in the image to account for the change.

CHAPTER
5

Manipulating Selections

Making a selection defines a specific area of your Photoshop image. This chapter shows you how to move, stretch, erase, and manipulate your selections in a variety of ways.

You can move a selection by using the Move tool, which enables you to rearrange elements of your image.

You can place elements of your image either in the background or in layers. For details about layers, see Chapter 8.

Move a Selection

MOVE A SELECTED OBJECT IN THE BACKGROUND

① Click the Background layer in the Layers palette.

If you start with a newly scanned image, Photoshop makes the Background layer the only layer.

② Make a selection with a selection tool.

Note: See Chapter 4 for more about the selection tools, and Chapter 8 for more about layers.

③ Click the **Move** tool ().

④ Click inside the selection and drag.

● Photoshop fills the original location of the object with the current background color.

● In this example, white is the default background color.

MOVE A SELECTED OBJECT IN A LAYER

1. Click a layer in the Layers palette.

2. Make a selection with a selection tool.

Note: See Chapter 4 for more about the selection tools, and Chapter 8 for more about layers.

3. Click .

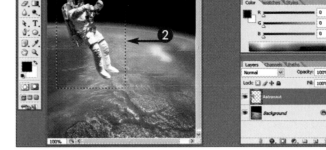

4. Click inside the selection and drag.

Photoshop moves the selection in the layer.

Photoshop fills the original location of the object with transparent pixels.

Note: Unlike the background — Photoshop's opaque default layer — layers can include transparent pixels.

TIPS

How do I move a selection in a straight line?

Press and hold down the Shift key while you drag with the **Move** tool (). Doing so constrains the movement of your object horizontally, vertically, or diagonally — depending on the direction you drag.

How do I move several layers at a time?

You can link the layers that you want to move, select one of the linked layers, and then move them all with the Move tool. For more information, see Chapter 8.

Copy and Paste a Selection

You can copy a selection and make a duplicate of it somewhere else in the image.

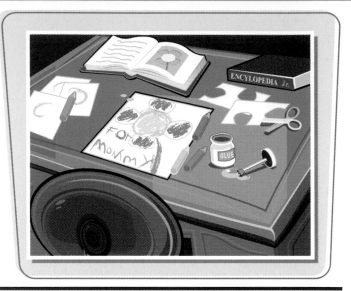

Copy and Paste a Selection

USING THE KEYBOARD AND MOUSE

① Make a selection with a selection tool.

Note: See Chapter 4 for more about the selection tools.

② Click 🔁.

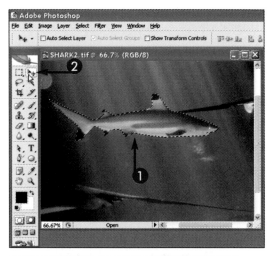

③ Press Alt (Option on the Mac) while you click and drag the object.

④ Release the mouse button to "drop" the selection.

Photoshop creates a duplicate of the object, which appears in the new location.

The copied pixels stay in the same layer from which they were copied.

USING THE COPY AND PASTE COMMANDS

1 Make a selection with a selection tool.

Note: See Chapter 4 for more about the selection tools.

2 Click **Edit**.

3 Click **Copy**.

4 Using a selection tool, select where you want to paste the copied element.

If you do not select an area, Photoshop pastes the copy over the original.

5 Click **Edit**.

6 Click **Paste**.

● Photoshop pastes the copy into a new layer, which you can now move independently of the original image.

Note: See the section "Move a Selection" for more about moving your image.

How can I copy a selection from one window to another?

Click ▶✛ and click and drag your selection from one window to another. You can also copy selections between windows using the **Copy** and **Paste** commands in the **Edit** menu.

How can I copy content from multiple layers at once?

If your selection overlaps several layers in your image, you can click **Edit** and then **Copy Merged** to copy the content from all of them. Using the regular Copy command will only copy from the selected layer. For more about layers, see Chapter 8.

Delete a Selection

You can delete a selection to remove an element from your image.

1 Make a selection with a selection tool.

Note: See Chapter 4 for more about the selection tools.

2 Press Delete.

Photoshop deletes the selection.

If you are working in the Background layer, the empty area fills with the background color – in this example, white, the default background color.

If you are working in a layer other than the Background layer, deleting an object turns the selected pixels transparent.

You can rotate a selection to tilt it or turn it upside down in your image.

Rotate a Selection

① Make a selection with a selection tool.

Note: See Chapter 4 for more about the selection tools.

② Click **Edit**.

③ Click **Transform**.

④ Click **Rotate**.

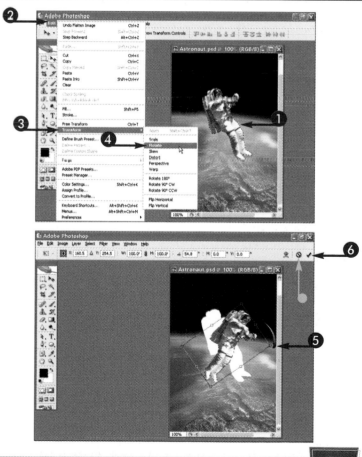

A *bounding box*, a rectangular box with handles on the sides and corners, surrounds the object.

⑤ Click and drag to the side of the object.

The object rotates.

⑥ Click ✓ or press Enter (Return on the Mac) to apply the rotation.

● You can click Ⓞ or press Esc (⌘ + . on the Mac) to cancel.

Scale a Selection

You can scale a selection to make it larger or smaller. By scaling, you can emphasize parts of your image.

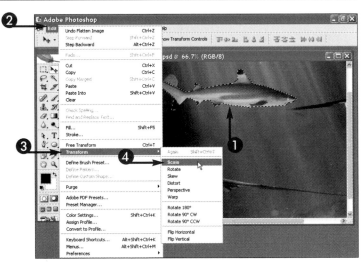

Scale a Selection

① Make a selection with a selection tool.

Note: See Chapter 4 for more about the selection tools.

② Click **Edit**.

③ Click **Transform**.

④ Click **Scale**.

A rectangular bounding box with handles on the sides and corners surrounds the object.

⑤ Click and drag a corner handle to scale both the horizontal and vertical axes.

6 Click and drag a side handle to scale one axis at a time.

7 To apply the scaling, click ☑ or press **Enter** (**Return** on the Mac).

● To cancel, you can click ◯ or press **Esc** (⌘ + . on the Mac).

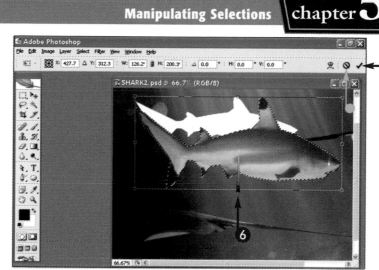

Photoshop scales the object to the new dimensions.

How do I scale both dimensions proportionally?

Hold down **Shift** while you scale your selection. The two axes of your selection grow or shrink proportionally. Photoshop does not distort your image.

Skew or Distort a Selection

You can transform a selection using the Skew or Distort command. This enables you to stretch elements in your image into interesting shapes.

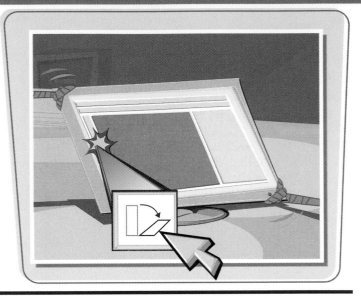

Skew or Distort a Selection

SKEW A SELECTION

① Make a selection with a selection tool.

Note: See Chapter 4 for more about the selection tools.

② Click **Edit**.

③ Click **Transform**.

④ Click **Skew**.

● A rectangular bounding box with handles on the sides and corners surrounds the object.

⑤ Click and drag a handle to skew the object.

Because the Skew command works along a single axis, you can drag either horizontally or vertically.

⑥ To apply the skewing, click ☑ or press Enter (Return on the Mac).

● To cancel, you can click Ⓞ or press Esc (⌘ + . on the Mac).

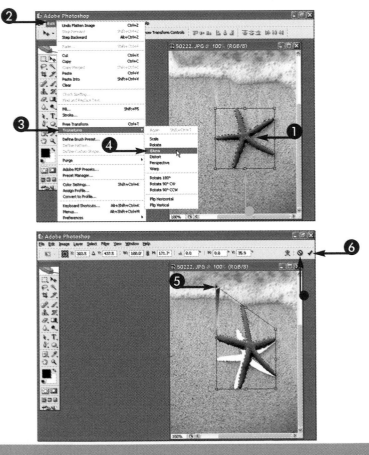

DISTORT A SELECTION

1 Make a selection with a selection tool.

Note: See Chapter 4 for more about the selection tools.

2 Click **Edit**.

3 Click **Transform**.

4 Click **Distort**.

● A rectangular bounding box with handles on the sides and corners surrounds the object.

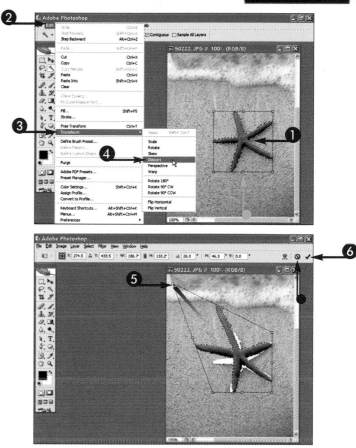

5 Click and drag a handle to distort the object.

The Distort command works independently of the selection's different axes: You can drag a handle both vertically and horizontally.

6 To apply the distortion, click ✓ or press Enter (Return on a Mac).

● To cancel, you can click ⊘ or press Esc (⌘ + . on a Mac).

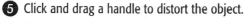

How can I undo my skewing or distortion?

You can click **Edit** and then **Undo** to undo the last handle adjustment you made. This is an alternative to clicking ⊘, which cancels the entire Skew or Distort command.

How can I flip my image horizontally or vertically?

You can click **Edit, Transform,** and then **Flip Horizontal** or **Flip Vertical**. The Flip Horizontal command makes a selection look like its mirror image.

Feather the Border of a Selection

You can feather a selection's border to create soft edges.

To soften edges, you must first select an object, feather the selection border, and then delete the part of the image that surrounds your selection.

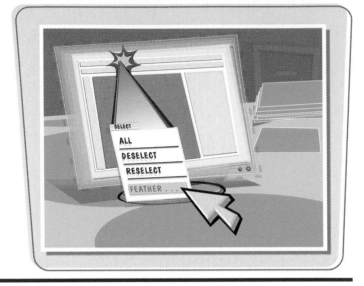

Feather the Border of a Selection

SELECT AND FEATHER THE IMAGE

1. Make a selection with a selection tool.

Note: See Chapter 4 for more about the selection tools.

2. Click **Select**.

3. Click **Feather**.

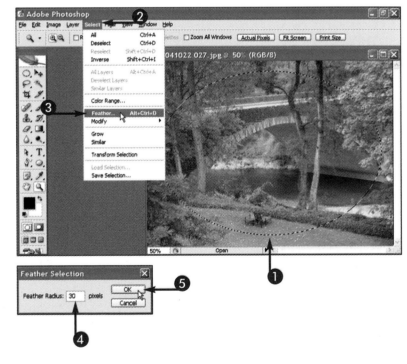

The Feather Selection dialog box appears.

4. Type a pixel value between **0.2** and **250** to determine the softness of the edge; the larger the number, the wider the softened edge.

5. Click **OK**.

DELETE THE SURROUNDING BACKGROUND

6 Click **Select**.

7 Click **Inverse**.

The selection inverts but remains feathered.

8 Press **Backspace** (**Delete** on a Mac).

You can now see the effect of the feathering.

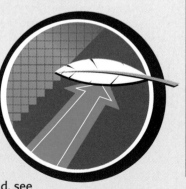

What happens if I feather a selection and then apply a command to it?

Photoshop applies the command only partially to pixels near the edge of the selection. For example, if you are removing color from a selection using the Hue/Saturation command, color at the feathered edge of the selection is only partially removed. For more information about the Hue/Saturation command, see Chapter 7.

Is there another way to feather my selection?

When selecting with the Marquee or Lasso tool, you can create a feathered selection by first typing a pixel value greater than 0 in the Feather text field in the Options bar. Your resulting selection will have a feathered edge. Note that you must specify a **Feather** value before making the selection.

Extract an Object

You can remove objects in an image from their backgrounds using the Extract command. This command can be more convenient than the Lasso tool for removing an object.

Extract an Object

1 Click **Filter**.

2 Click **Extract**.

Photoshop displays the image in the Extract dialog box.

If you make a selection before you perform the Extract command, only the selection is displayed.

3 Click the **Edge Highlighter** tool ().

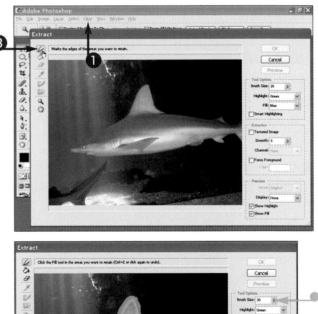

4 Highlight the edge of the object that you want to extract from the background.

The highlighting should overlay both the object and the background evenly.

● You can change the size of the highlighter.

For defined edges, use a smaller brush size; for fuzzier edges, use a larger brush size.

5 Click the Fill tool (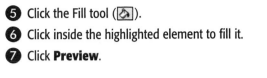).

6 Click inside the highlighted element to fill it.

7 Click **Preview**.

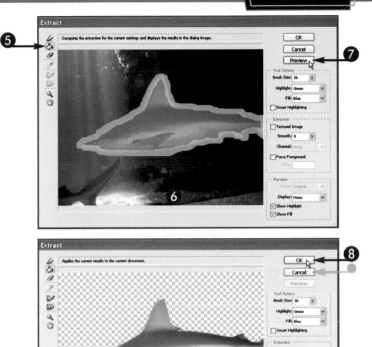

The object is extracted from the background.

8 Click **OK**.

Photoshop returns you to the original image window with the element extracted.

● You can click **Cancel** to return without extracting.

TIP

My extraction has rough edges. What can I do?

You can improve a less-than-perfect extraction by clicking the **Show** ☑ (⦂ on a Mac) and then **Original** in the Extract dialog box. Click **Show Highlight** and **Show Fill** (🖉 changes to ☐). You can then edit your work. Click 🖉 to erase any errant highlighting, and then rehighlight those edges with the highlighter (🖉). Adjusting the value from 0 to 100 in the Smooth box can also help fine-tune the extraction process.

Create Vanishing Point Planes

You can model the 3-D characteristics of flat objects in your image by creating planes with the Vanishing Point tool. This can be useful if you are working with objects such as the sides of buildings, interior walls, or table surfaces.

After you create Vanishing Point planes, you can apply special Photoshop commands. See "Copy between Vanishing Point Planes" for details.

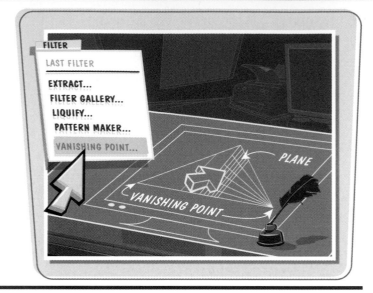

Create Vanishing Point Planes

① Open an image that includes flat surfaces.

Note: See Chapter 1 for more about opening an image.

② Click **Filter**.

③ Click **Vanishing Point**.

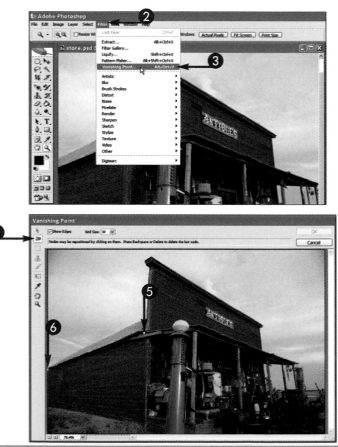

The Vanishing Point dialog box opens.

④ Click the **Create Plane** tool (🔲).

⑤ Click to mark a corner of a plane.

⑥ Click a second time to mark another corner.

Photoshop connects the points to create a plane edge.

7 Click two more times to mark the final two corners of the plane.

Photoshop creates the Vanishing Point plane.

● You can use the **Edit Plane** tool () to move a plane or adjust its corners or sides.

8 Click to reselect it.

9 Click four more times to create another Vanishing Point plane.

Photoshop creates the Vanishing Point plane. The plane is oriented differently from the first.

● To delete a plane, you can select a plane with and press **Backspace** (**Delete** on a Mac).

10 Click **OK**.

Photoshop saves your work and closes the dialog box.

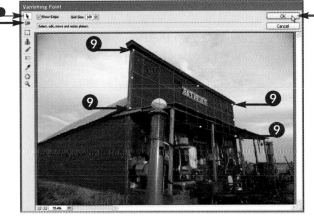

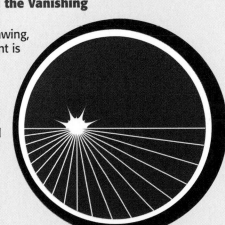

TIP

Why is it called the Vanishing Point tool?

In perspective drawing, the vanishing point is the point on the horizon where receding parallel lines appear to meet. Photoshop uses such parallel lines to represent the planes in the Vanishing Point dialog box.

Copy between Vanishing Point Planes

You can copy an object between two Vanishing Point planes. Photoshop transforms the object as you move it so that it conforms to the orientation of the current plane.

Copy between Vanishing Point Planes

① Create Vanishing Point planes in your image.

Note: For details, see the section "Create Vanishing Point Planes."

② Click **Filter**.

③ Click **Vanishing Point**.

The Vanishing Point dialog box opens, displaying the different planes.

④ Click the **Rectangular Marquee** tool (▢).

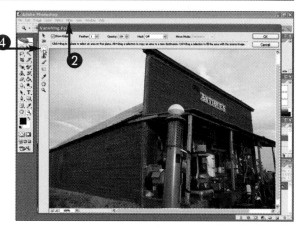

⑤ Click and drag to select an object inside a plane.

Photoshop draws a marquee whose angles are proportional to the plane.

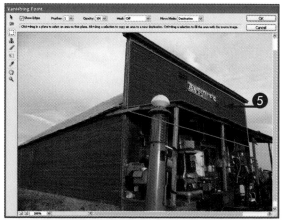

6 Press and hold **Alt** (**Option** on a Mac).

7 Click and drag the selection from one plane to another.

Photoshop transforms the selection to orient it with the destination plane.

8 Click the **Transform** tool ().

9 Click **Flip** (☐ changes to ☑) to flip the selection horizontally.

● You can click the **Flop** option (☐ changes to ☑) to flip the selection vertically.

10 Click **OK**.

Photoshop saves your work and closes the dialog box.

What does the Paintbrush tool () do in the Vanishing Point dialog box?

Like the normal Paintbrush, it applies the foreground color to objects in your image; but in the Vanishing Point dialog box, the brush shape conforms to the plane in which you paint. You can control the characteristics of the brush with the settings at the top of the dialog box.

What does the Stamp tool () do in the Vanishing Point dialog box?

It enables you to clone content from one Vanishing Point plane to another. The cloned pixels conform to the shape of the current plane.

CHAPTER 6

Painting and Drawing with Color

Want to add splashes, streaks, or solid areas of color to your image? Photoshop offers a variety of tools with which you can add almost any color imaginable. This chapter introduces you to those tools and shows you how to choose your colors.

Select the Foreground and Background Colors

You can select two colors to work with at a time in Photoshop — a foreground color and a background color. Painting tools such as the Paintbrush apply the foreground color. You apply the background color when you use the Eraser tool, enlarge the image canvas, or cut pieces out of your image.

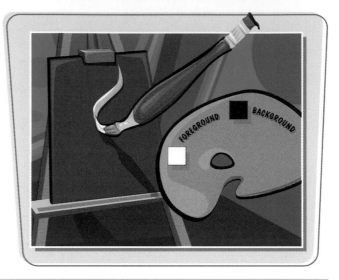

Select the Foreground and Background Colors

SELECT THE FOREGROUND COLOR

① Click the **Foreground Color** box.

The Color Picker dialog box appears.

● To change the range of colors that appears in the color box, click and drag the slider (▷).

② Click the color you want as the foreground color in the color box.

③ Click **OK**.

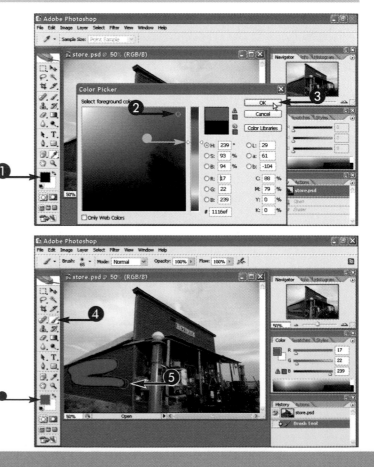

● The selected color appears in the **Foreground Color** box.

④ Click a painting tool in the toolbox.

This example uses the **Paintbrush** tool (✐).

Note: For more about painting tools, see the section "Using the Paintbrush Tool."

⑤ Click and drag to apply the color.

SELECT THE BACKGROUND COLOR

1 Click the **Background Color** box.

● To change the range of colors that appears in the color box, click and drag ▷.

2 To select a background color, click the color you want in the color box.

3 Click **OK**.

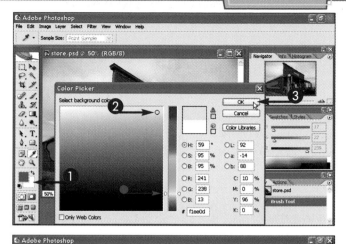

4 Click the **Eraser** tool (🖌️).

5 Click and drag your cursor (○).

The tool "erases" by painting with the background color.

Note: Painting occurs only in the Background layer; in other layers, the eraser turns pixels transparent. See Chapter 8 for a full discussion of layers.

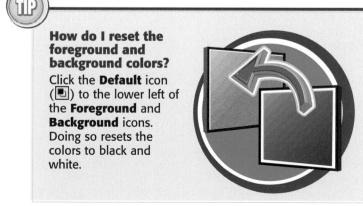

How do I reset the foreground and background colors?

Click the **Default** icon (🔳) to the lower left of the **Foreground** and **Background** icons. Doing so resets the colors to black and white.

Select a
Web-Safe Color

You can select one of the 216 Web-safe colors as a foreground or background color. A Web-safe color displays accurately in all Web browsers, no matter what type of color monitor or operating system a user has.

See Chapter 14 for information about saving images for the Web.

Select a Web-Safe Color

① Click the **Foreground Color** box.

Alternatively, to select a Web-safe background color, you can click the **Background Color** box.

The Color Picker dialog box appears.

② Click the **Only Web Colors** option (☐ changes to ☑).

Photoshop displays only Web-safe colors in the Color Picker window.

③ Click a color.

● The hex-code value for the selected color appears here.

④ Click **OK**.

● The color appears in the Foreground Color box.

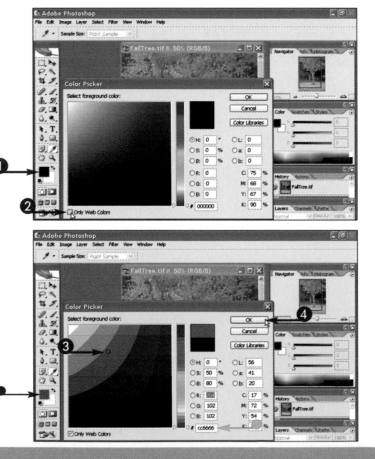

You can select a color from an open image with the Eyedropper tool. The Eyedropper tool enables you to paint using a color already present in your image.

Select a Color with the Eyedropper Tool

① Click the **Eyedropper** tool (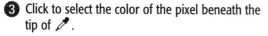).

② Place 🖊 over your image.

● If you click the **Info** palette tab, you can see color values as you move 🖊 .

③ Click to select the color of the pixel beneath the tip of 🖊 .

● The color becomes the new foreground color.

To select a new background color, you can press **Alt** (**Option** on the Mac) as you click in step **3**.

Select a Color with the Swatches Palette

You can select a color with the Swatches palette. The Swatches palette lets you choose from a small set of commonly used colors.

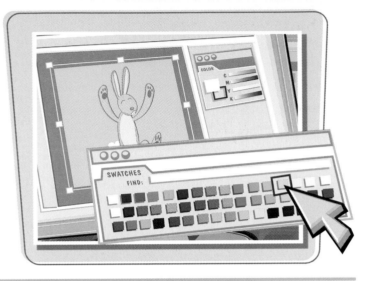

① Click the **Swatches** palette tab.

② Place your cursor over a color swatch.

   ◊ changes to 🖋.

③ Click a color swatch to select a foreground color.

● The color becomes the new foreground color.

   To select a background color, press Alt (Option on a Mac) as you click in step 3.

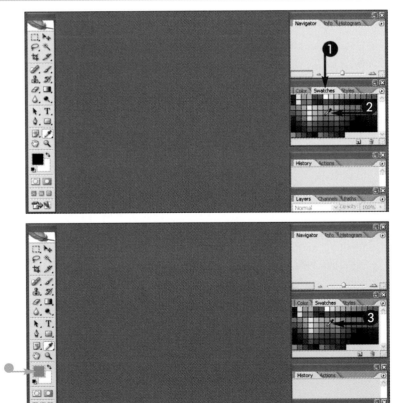

Add a Color to the Swatches Palette

You can add custom colors to the Swatches palette. This enables you to easily select these colors later.

Add a Color to the Swatches Palette

1. Click 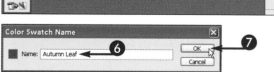.

2. Click inside the image to select a color.

   ● The color appears in the Foreground Color box.

3. Click the **Swatches** palette tab.

4. Place ✐ over an empty area of the Swatches palette (✐ changes to ◇).

5. Click to add the color.

The Color Swatch Name dialog box appears.

6. Type a name for the new color swatch.

7. Click **OK**.

   Photoshop adds the color as a new swatch.

   You can remove a swatch by clicking it and dragging it to the **Trash** icon (🗑).

Using the Paintbrush Tool

You can use the Paintbrush tool to add color to your image. You may find the Paintbrush useful for applying bands of color.

To limit where the Paintbrush applies color, create a selection before painting. For details, see Chapter 4.

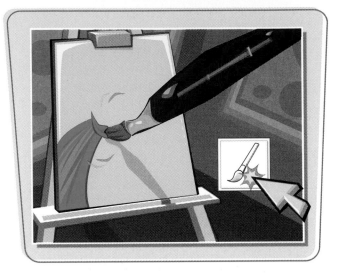

① Click the .

② Click the **Foreground Color** box to select a color with which to paint.

Note: For details, see the section "Select the Foreground and Background Colors."

③ Click the **Brush** ⊡ and select a brush size and type.

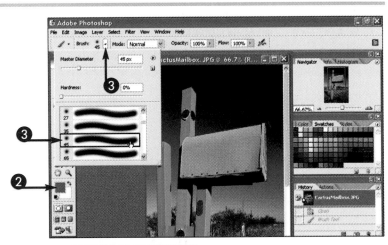

④ Click and drag to apply the foreground color to the image.

To undo the most recent brush stroke, you can click **Edit** and then **Undo Paintbrush**.

Note: To undo more than one brush stroke, see Chapter 2 for more about the History palette.

⑤ Type a percentage value to change the opacity of the brush strokes.

Alternatively, you can click the **Opacity** and adjust the slider.

⑥ Click and drag to apply the semitransparent paintbrush.

⑦ Type a percentage value to change how much color the brush applies.

Alternatively, you can click the **Flow** and adjust the slider.

⑧ Click and drag to apply the customized paintbrush.

Photoshop applies color per your specifications.

TIP

What is the Airbrush tool?

You can convert your paintbrush to an airbrush by clicking the **Airbrush** button () in the Options bar. The Airbrush paints soft lines that get darker the longer you hold down your mouse button.

You can select from a variety of predefined brush styles to apply color in different ways. The types of brushes available include calligraphic brushes, texture brushes, and brushes that enable you to add drop shadows to objects.

Change Brush Styles

① Click 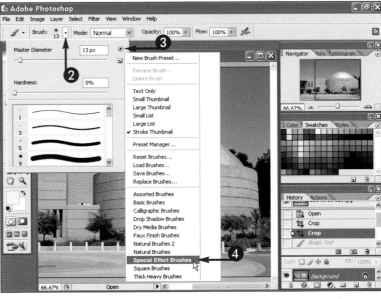.

② Click the **Brush** .

③ Click .

The Brush menu appears.

④ Click a set of brushes.

A dialog box appears asking if you want to replace your brushes.

⑤ Click **OK**.

● To add the set of brushes to the currently displayed set, click **Append**.

If a dialog box appears asking if you want to save the current brush set, click **No**.

Note: You can reset your brushes to the original set by selecting **Reset Brushes** from the **Brush** menu.

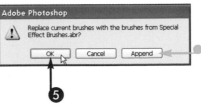

The new set appears in the Brush list.

● You can click and drag 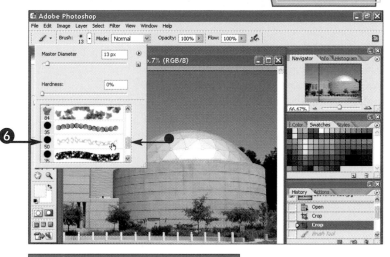 to view all the brush styles.

6 Click a brush style to select it.

7 Click and drag to apply the new paintbrush.

Photoshop applies color with the brush.

TIP

How can I give my brush strokes a scattered appearance?

Open the Brushes palette by clicking **Window** and then **Brushes**. Click the **Scattering** option (☐ changes to ☑). Photoshop displays an example of the custom brush stroke at the bottom of the palette. You can change the scattering settings with the controls on the right side of the palette. After closing the Brushes palette, you can apply the customized brush like any other brush.

Create a Custom Brush

You can use the Brushes palette to create one-of-a-kind brushes of varying sizes and shapes. You can even specify a brush shape that changes as it paints, to generate a random design.

① Click ✏.

② Click the **Brush** ☐ and select a brush style to use as a starting point for your custom brush.

③ Click the **Toggle Brushes** button (☐).

The Brushes palette opens.

④ Click **Brush Tip Shape**.

⑤ Click and drag the **Diameter** slider (☐) to change the brush size.

⑥ Type a Roundness value between **0%** and **100%.**

The lower the number, the more oval the brush.

You can adjust other settings to further define the tip shape.

⑦ Click **Shape Dynamics** (☐ changes to ☑).

⑧ Click and drag the **Size Jitter** 🔲 to specify the amount your brush varies in size as it paints.

⑨ Click and drag the **Minimum Diameter** 🔲 to specify the smallest size to which the brush scales when Size Jitter is enabled.

⑩ Click and drag the other sliders to control how the brush angle and roundness change.

● You can click other categories to define additional settings.

⑪ Click the **Close** button (⊠) (⊙ on a Mac) to close the Brushes palette.

⑫ Click and drag inside the image.

Photoshop applies the custom brush.

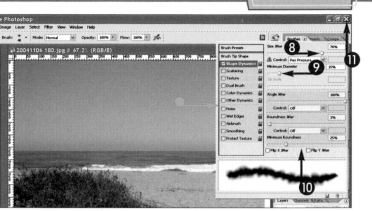

TIP

How do I save my custom brush in the Brush drop-down menu?

In the Brushes palette, click the **Brush** ⬚ and then click **New Brush Preset**. A dialog box appears and asks you to name your custom brush. Type a name and then click **OK** to add your brush to the Brush menu.

Using the Pencil Tool

You can use the Pencil tool to draw hard-edged lines of color. The Pencil tool's lines are more jagged than those of the paintbrush.

① Click and hold ✐.

② From the list that appears, select the **Pencil Tool** (✐).

③ Click the **Foreground Color** box to select a color to draw with.

Note: For details, see the section "Select the Foreground and Background Colors."

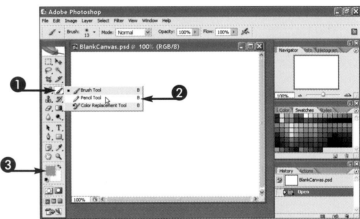

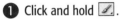

④ Click the **Brush** ⬚.

⑤ Click to select a brush size and type.

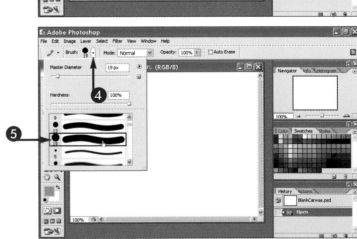

6 Click and drag to apply the foreground color to the image.

● You can type an opacity value below 100% to draw semitransparent lines.

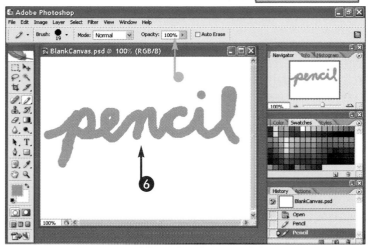

DRAW STRAIGHT LINES

7 Press and hold Shift.

8 Click several places inside your image, without dragging.

Photoshop draws straight lines between the clicked points.

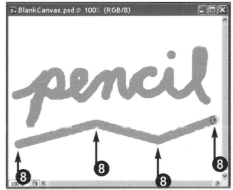

TIP

What is the Auto Erase function?

If you click **Auto Erase** (☐ changes to ☑) in the Options bar, the Pencil tool acts like an eraser when you click and drag it over the foreground color in your image. If you first click colors other than the foreground color, it acts like a regular pencil. For more about the Eraser tool, see the section "Using the Eraser" in this chapter.

Apply a Gradient

You can apply a gradient, which is a transition from one color to another. This can give objects or areas in your image a shaded or 3-D look.

For another way to add a gradient to your image, see Chapter 8.

Apply a Gradient

① Make a selection.

Note: See Chapter 4 for more about making selections.

② Click the **Gradient** tool (▨).

● A linear gradient is the default.

You can select different geometries in the Options bar.

③ Click the gradient swatch.

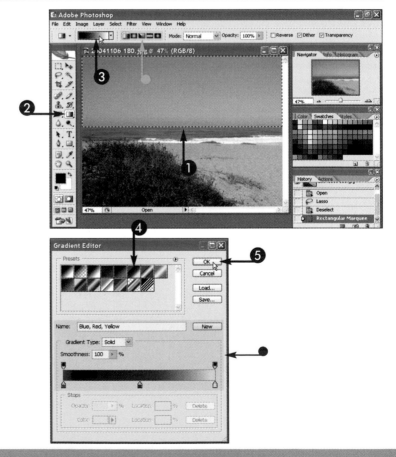

The Gradient Editor appears.

④ Select a gradient type from the preset box.

● Photoshop shows the settings for the selected gradient below.

You can customize the gradient using the settings.

⑤ Click **OK**.

6 Click and drag inside the selection.

Note: This defines the direction and transition of the gradient. Dragging a long line with the tool produces a gradual transition. Dragging a short line with the tool produces an abrupt transition.

● Photoshop generates a gradient inside the selection.

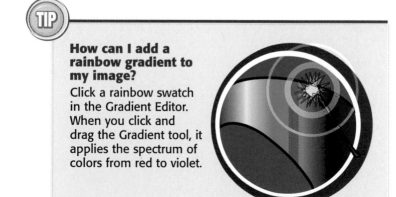

TIP

How can I add a rainbow gradient to my image?

Click a rainbow swatch in the Gradient Editor. When you click and drag the Gradient tool, it applies the spectrum of colors from red to violet.

Using the Paint Bucket Tool

You can fill areas in your image with solid color using the Paint Bucket tool.

The Paint Bucket tool affects only adjacent pixels in the image. You can set the Paint Bucket's Tolerance value to determine what range of colors the paint bucket affects in the image when you apply it.

To fill the pixels of a selected area, rather than just adjacent pixels, see the section "Fill a Selection."

Using the Paint Bucket Tool

① Click and hold 🔲.

② From the list that appears, select **Paint Bucket Tool** (🪣).

③ Click the **Foreground Color** box to select a color for painting.

Note: For details, see the section "Select the Foreground and Background Colors."

④ Type a Tolerance value from **0** to **255**.

With a low value, the tool fills only adjacent colors that are very similar to that of the clicked pixel.

A high value fills a broader range of colors.

⑤ Click inside the image.

Photoshop fills an area of the image with the foreground color.

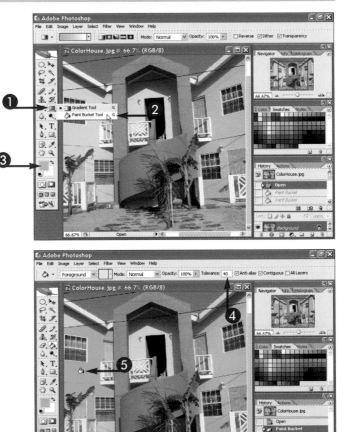

ADJUST OPACITY

6 To fill an area with a semitransparent color, type a percentage value of less than 100 in the Opacity field.

7 Click inside the image.

Photoshop fills an area with see-through paint.

CONSTRAIN THE COLOR

8 To constrain where you apply the color, make a selection before clicking.

In this example, the opacity was reset to 100%.

9 Click inside the selection.

The fill effect stays within the boundary of the selection.

TIP

How can I reset a tool to its default settings?

Right-click (Ctrl +click) the tool's icon on the far left side of the Options bar and select **Reset Tool** from the menu that appears.

Fill a Selection

You can fill a selection using the Fill command. The Fill command is an alternative to the Paint Bucket tool. The Fill command differs from the Paint Bucket tool in that it fills the entire selected area, not just adjacent pixels based on a tolerance value.

See the section "Using the Paint Bucket Tool" if you want to fill adjacent pixels rather than a selected area.

Fill a Selection

① Define the area you want to fill using a selection tool.

Note: See Chapter 4 for more about using the selection tools.

② Click **Edit**.

③ Click **Fill**.

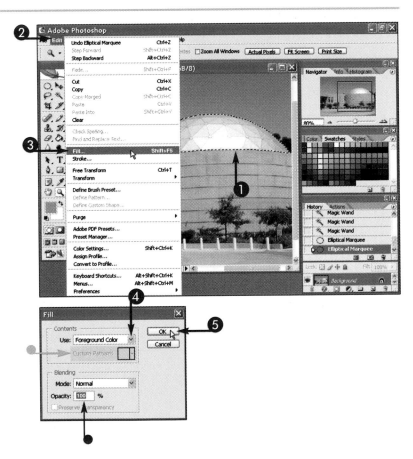

④ Click here and select a fill option.

● To use the Custom Pattern option, click the **Rectangular Marquee** tool () and select an area of the image to use as a fill pattern. Next, click **Edit** and then **Define Pattern**.

● You can decrease the opacity to fill with a semitransparent color or pattern.

⑤ Click **OK**.

● Photoshop fills the area.

You can select other areas and fill them with different colors.

● This example uses a fill with the background color set to 60% opacity.

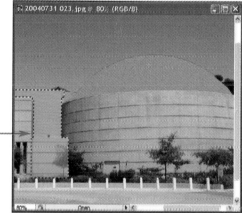

TIPS

How do I apply a "ghosted" white layer over part of an image?

Use a selection tool to define the area of the image that you want to cover. Then apply the Fill command with white selected and the opacity set to less than 50%.

What does the Preserve Transparency option in the Fill dialog box do?

If you click **Preserve Transparency** (☐ changes to ☑) and perform a fill, Photoshop only fills pixels that are not transparent in the layer; it leaves transparent pixels alone. This option enables you to easily color objects that exist by themselves in a layer.

Stroke a Selection

You can use the Stroke command to draw a line along the edge of a selection. This can help you highlight objects in your image.

Stroke a Selection

① Select an area of the image with a selection tool.

Note: See Chapter 4 for more about using the selection tools.

② Click **Edit**.

③ Click **Stroke**.

The Stroke dialog box appears.

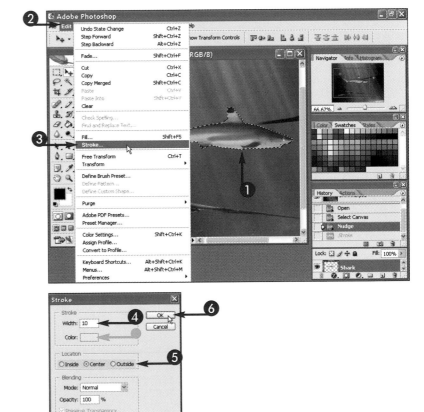

④ Type a width in pixels.

⑤ Click a location option (○ changes to ⊙).

You can click **Inside** to stroke a line on the inside of the selection, **Center** to stroke a line straddling the selection, or **Outside** to stroke a line on the outside of the selection

● You can click the **Color** box to define the color of the stroke.

⑥ Click **OK**.

● Photoshop strokes a line along the selection.

You can select other areas and stroke them using different settings.

● This stroke was applied to the outside of the selection at 50% opacity.

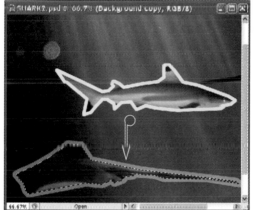

TIP

How do I add a colored border to my image?
Click **Select** and then **All**. Apply the Stroke command, clicking **Inside** as the Location (○ changes to ◉). Photoshop adds a border to the image.

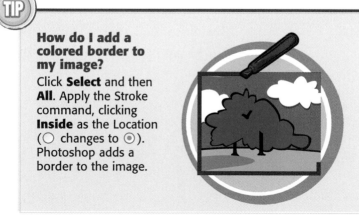

Using the Clone Stamp

You can clean up small flaws or erase elements in your image with the Clone Stamp tool. This tool copies information from one area of an image to another.

For other ways to correct defects in your image, see the sections "Using the Healing Brush" and "Using the Patch Tool."

Using the Clone Stamp

① Click the **Clone Stamp** tool (🔳).

② Click the **Brush** 🔽 and select a brush size and type.

③ Press and hold **Alt** (**Option** on a Mac) and click the area of the image from which you want to copy.

You can specify an opacity of less than 100%.

You can **Alt**-click (**Option**-click on a Mac) another open image.

This example uses the tool to select an empty area of the sky.

④ Release **Alt** (**Option** on a Mac) .

⑤ Click and drag to apply the Clone Stamp.

Photoshop copies the previously clicked area to where you click and drag.

⑥ Click and drag repeatedly over the image to achieve the desired effect.

As you apply the tool, you can press **Alt** (**Option** on a Mac) and click again to select a different area from which to copy.

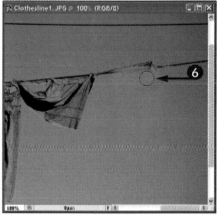

TIP

How can I make the Clone Stamp's effects look seamless?

To erase elements from your image with the Clone Stamp without leaving a trace, try the following:

● Clone between areas of similar color and texture.

● To apply the clone stamp more subtly, lower its opacity in the Options bar.

● After you click the **Brush** ⬚, choose a soft-edged brush shape.

Using the Pattern Stamp

You can paint with a pattern using the Pattern Stamp tool. This tool gives you a free-form way to add repeating elements to your images.

SELECT A PATTERN

1. Click and hold .

2. From the list that appears, select the **Pattern Stamp** tool (📑).

3. Click the **Brush** ⬚.

4. Select a brush size and type.

5. Click the Pattern ⬚.

6. Select a pattern to apply.

● You can click **Aligned** (☐ changes to ☑) to make your strokes paint the pattern as contiguous tiles.

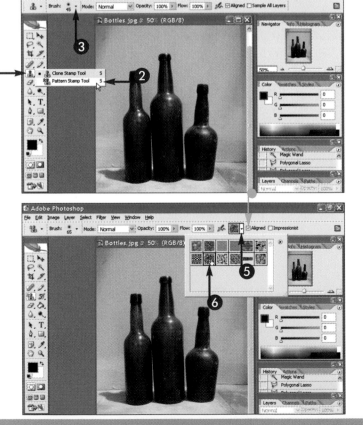

7 Click and drag to apply the pattern.

Photoshop applies the pattern wherever you click and drag.

APPLY A DIFFERENT OPACITY

8 Type a value of less than **100** in the Opacity box.

9 Click and drag inside the selection to apply the pattern.

Decreasing the opacity causes the brush to apply a semitransparent pattern.

TIP

How do I define my own custom patterns?

Select what you want to use as a pattern with the **Rectangular Marquee** tool (▢), click **Edit**, and then click **Define Pattern**. A dialog box appears and asks you to name the new pattern. You can click **OK** to add the new pattern to the Pattern menu. For more about the Rectangular Marquee tool and how to select objects, see Chapter 4.

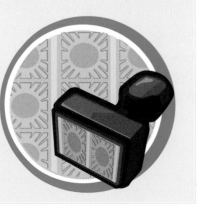

Using the Healing Brush

You can correct defects in your image using the Healing Brush. The Healing Brush is similar to the Clone Stamp in that it copies pixels from one area of the image to another. However, the Healing Brush takes into account the texture and lighting of the image as it works, which can make its modifications more convincing.

Using the Healing Brush

① Click and hold the **Spot Healing Brush** tool (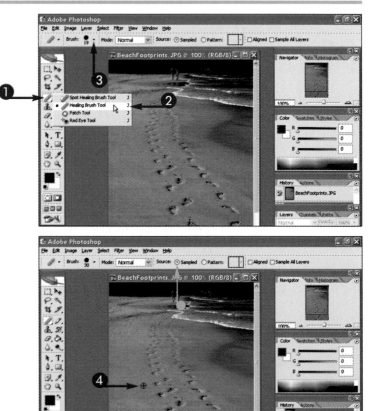).

② From the list that appears, click **Healing Brush Tool**.

③ Click the **Brush** ⊙ and specify your brush settings.

● Make sure the **Sampled** option is selected (○ changes to ◉).

④ Press and hold Alt (Option on a Mac) and click the area of the image you want to heal with.

5 Release the `Alt` (`Option` on a Mac) key.

6 Click and drag inside the selection to apply the Healing Brush.

Photoshop copies the selected area wherever you click and drag.

7 Stop dragging and release the mouse button.

Photoshop adjusts the copied pixels to account for the lighting and texture present in the image.

TIP

How does the Spot Healing Brush tool work?

The **Spot Healing Brush** ( ) is a less interactive version of the **Healing Brush** ( ). With the Brush settings, you specify the diameter of the area that you want to select. When you click an imperfection in your image, Photoshop attempts to automatically heal the selected area. It replaces the imperfection inside the selected area with the surrounding colors. If you click the **Create Texture** option (○ changes to ⊙), the tool attempts to mimic the texture of the selected area as well.

Using the Patch Tool

The Patch tool enables you to correct defects in your image by selecting them and dragging the selection to an unflawed area of the image. This can be useful if a large part of your image is free of flaws.

For other ways to correct defects in your image, see the sections "Using the Clone Stamp" and "Using the Healing Brush."

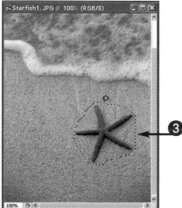

Using the Patch Tool

① Click 🖊.

② From the list that appears, click **Patch Tool** (🔘).

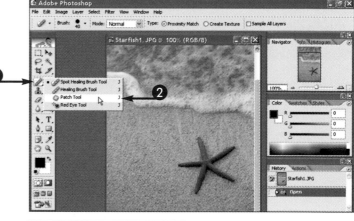

③ Click and drag to select the part of your image that contains the defects that you want to patch.

When you are making selections, the Patch tool works similarly to the Lasso tool.

Note: *See Chapter 4 for more about the Lasso tool.*

④ Click inside the selection and drag it to an area that does not have defects.

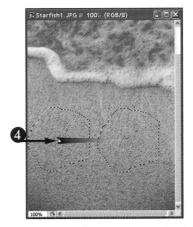

Photoshop uses pixels from the destination selection to patch the defects in the source selection.

● You can click the **Destination** option (○ changes to ◉) to patch defects in the reverse order — flaws in the destination selection are corrected with the pixels from the source selection.

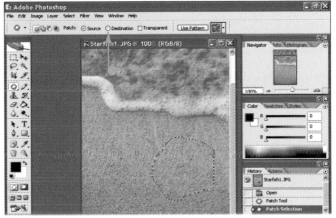

TIP

How does the Patch tool determine what are defects in my selection?

It does this by comparing the colors and textures in the two selections. The tool then tries to eliminate the differences — the defects — while retaining the overall color and texture.

Using the History Brush

You can use the History brush to paint a previous state of your image from the History palette into the current image. This can be useful if you want to revert just a part of your image.

① Click **Window**.

② Click **History**.

The History palette opens.

③ Click the **New Snapshot** button (▣) in the History palette.

● Photoshop puts a copy of the current state of the image into the History palette.

④ Modify your image to make it different from the newly created snapshot.

In this example, the image was desaturated by clicking **Image Adjustment**, and then **Desaturate**.

⑤ Click to the left of the snapshot to select it as the History brush source.

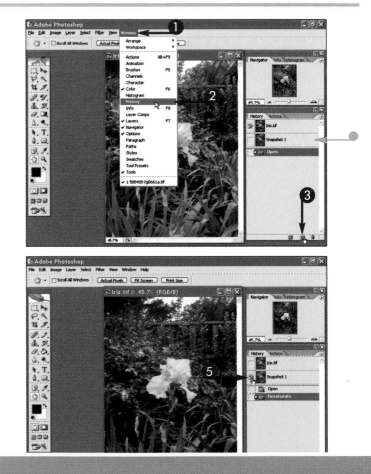

6 Click the **History** brush (🖌).

7 Click the **Brush** ⏷ and specify your brush settings.

8 Click and drag inside the image.

Pixels from the previous snapshot are painted into the image.

USING THE ART HISTORY BRUSH

1 Click and hold 🖌 and select the **Art History** brush (🖌).

With the Art History brush, you can paint in snapshot information with an added impressionistic effect.

2 Click the **Brush** ⏷ to specify the settings for the brush.

3 Click and drag across your image.

Photoshop applies an artistic effect.

TIP

How do I paint onto a blank image with the History brush?

Start with a photographic image, take a snapshot of it with the **New Snapshot** button (▢), and then fill the image with a solid color. See the section "Fill a Selection" for details. You can then use the **History** brush (🖌) to paint in the photographic content.

Using the
Eraser

You can delete elements from your images using the Eraser tool. This can be useful when you are trying to separate elements from their backgrounds.

IN THE BACKGROUND LAYER

1 Click the Background layer in the Layers palette.

If you start with a newly scanned image, the Background layer is the only layer.

Note: See Chapter 8 for more about layers.

2 Click ⬛.

3 Click the **Brush** ▯ and select a brush size and type.

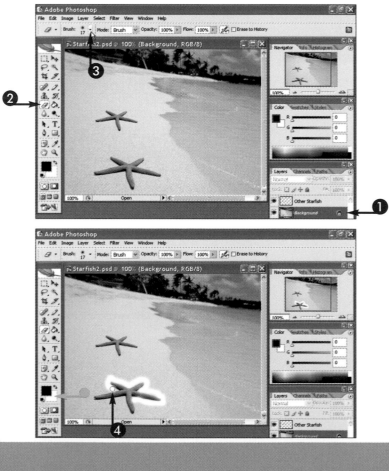

4 Click and drag inside the image.

● Photoshop erases the image by painting with the background color.

IN A REGULAR LAYER

① Click a nonbackground layer in the Layers palette.

Note: See Chapter 8 for more about layers.

② Click ☑.

③ Click the **Brush** ⊡ and select a brush size and type.

④ Click and drag inside the image.

Photoshop erases elements in the layer by making pixels transparent.

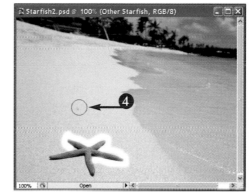

TIP

How can I quickly erase areas of similar color in my image?

If you click and hold ☑ in the toolbox, a list appears, and you can select the **Background Eraser** (☑) or the **Magic Eraser** (☑). The Background Eraser works by sampling the pixel color beneath the center of the brush and erasing similar colors that are underneath the brush. The Magic Eraser also samples the color beneath the cursor but erases similar pixels throughout the layer. You can adjust the tolerance of both tools in the Options bar to control how much they erase.

You can replace colors in your
image with the current foreground
color using the Color Replacement
tool. This gives you a free-form
way of recoloring objects in your
image, while keeping the shading
on the objects intact.

Replace a Color

① Click and hold .

② From the list that appears, select the **Color
Replacement** tool (▨).

③ Click the **Foreground Color** box to select a color for
painting.

*Note: For details, see the section "Select the Foreground and Background
Colors."*

④ Click the **Brush** ⬚ and select a brush size and type.

⑤ Click the **Sampling: Continuous** icon (▨).

Sampling: Continuous samples different colors to
replace as you paint.

● You can also click the **Sampling: Once** icon (▨),
which samples only the first color you click.

6 Type a tolerance from **1%** to **100%**.

The greater the tolerance, the greater the range of colors the tool replaces.

7 Click and drag in your image to replace color.

8 Continue to click and drag in your image.

Photoshop replaces more color.

TIP

How does the Color Replacement tool decide what colors to replace?

When you click inside your image, the **Color Replacement** tool (🖌) samples the color beneath the cross symbol at the center of the cursor. It then replaces any colors inside the brush that are similar to the sampled color. Photoshop determines similarity based on the Tolerance setting of the tool.

Fix Red Eye in a Photo

You can fix the red-eye effect that occurs in pictures taken with flash in low light by using the Red Eye tool. When applied to the eye of your subject, the tool replaces the reddish pixels in the area with pixels of a predefined color.

Fix Red Eye in a Photo

1 Click and hold 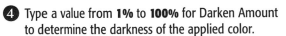.

2 From the list that appears, select **Red Eye Tool** (🔴).

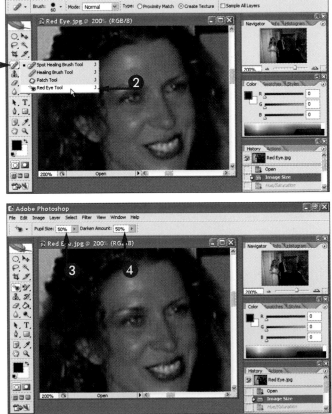

3 Type a value from **1** to **100** for Pupil Size to determine the size of the area affected.

4 Type a value from **1%** to **100%** for Darken Amount to determine the darkness of the applied color.

5 Click the center of a pupil.

Photoshop replaces the red pixels with a gray hue.

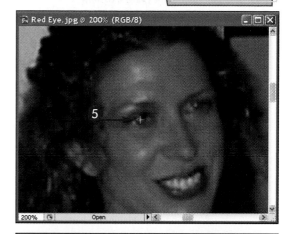

6 Click the other eye.

Photoshop fixes the other eye.

TIPS

What are alternatives to the Red Eye tool?

You can use the Color Replacement tool to fix red eye. First, select the red eye with the **Elliptical Marquee** tool (⬭). Select a grayish hue as your foreground color, and then apply the foreground color over the eye with the **Color Replacement** tool (✏️). For more on the Elliptical Marquee tool, see Chapter 4. For more on selecting a foreground color, see the section "Select the Foreground and Background Colors." For more on using the Color Replacement tool, see the section "Replace a Color."

What can cause problems for the Red Eye tool?

If your subject has a reddish skin tone in the photo, the Red Eye tool may apply color to more than just the eye. To improve the result, you can reduce the overall redness in your image by making hue and saturation adjustments. See Chapter 7 for more information.

CHAPTER 7

Adjusting Colors

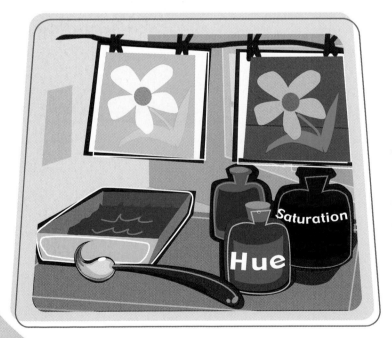

Do you want to fine-tune the colors in your image — darken them, lighten them, or remove them completely? This chapter introduces the tools that do the trick.

Change Brightness and Contrast

The Brightness/Contrast command provides a simple way to make adjustments to the highlights and shadows in your image.

To change the brightness or contrast of small parts of your image, use the Dodge or Burn tool. See the section "Using the Dodge and Burn Tools" for details.

If you make a selection before performing the Brightness/Contrast command, changes affect only the selected pixels. Similarly, if you have a multilayered image, your adjustments affect only the selected layer. See Chapter 4 to make a selection, and Chapter 8 for more about layers.

Change Brightness and Contrast

① Click **Image**.

② Click **Adjustments**.

③ Click **Brightness/Contrast**.

The Brightness/Contrast dialog box appears with sliders set to 0.

④ To display your adjustments in the image window as you make them, click the **Preview** option (☐ changes to ✓).

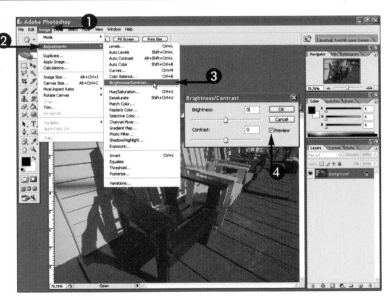

⑤ Click and drag the **Brightness** slider (◻).

Drag ◻ to the right to lighten the image, or to the left to darken the image.

● You can also lighten the image by typing a number from **1** to **100**, or darken the image by typing a (negative) number from **–1** to **–100**.

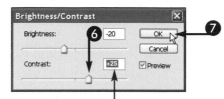

6 Click and drag the **Contrast** slider (▣).

Drag ▣ to the right to increase the contrast, or to the left to decrease the contrast.

Note: *Increasing contrast can bring out details in your image. Decreasing it can soften the details.*

● You can also increase the contrast by typing a number from **1** to **100**, or decrease the contrast by typing a (negative) number from **–1** to **–100**.

7 Click **OK**.

Photoshop applies the new brightness and contrast values.

TIP

How can I adjust the contrast of an image automatically?

Use Photoshop's **Auto Contrast** command. This converts the lightest pixels in the image to white and the darkest pixels in the image to black. Making the highlights brighter and the shadows darker boosts the contrast, which can improve the appearance of poorly exposed photographs.

1 Click **Image**.

2 Click **Adjustments**.

3 Click **Auto Contrast**.

Using the Dodge and Burn Tools

You can use the Dodge and Burn tools to brighten or darken a specific area of an image, respectively.

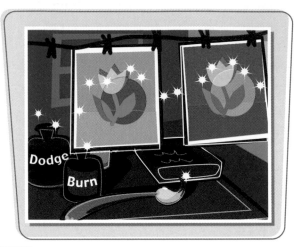

Dodge is a photographic term that describes the diffusing of light when developing a film negative. *Burn* is a photographic term that describes the focusing of light when developing a film negative.

These tools are an alternative to the Brightness/Contrast command, which affects the entire image. To brighten or darken the entire image, see the section "Change Brightness and Contrast."

Using the Dodge and Burn Tools

USING THE DODGE TOOL

① Click the **Dodge** tool (🔍).

② Click the **Brush** ⬚.

③ Click the brush you want to use.

● You can also select the range of colors you want to affect and the tool's exposure, or strength.

④ Click and drag over the area that you want to lighten.

Photoshop lightens the area.

USING THE BURN TOOL

1 Click and hold the 🔍.

2 Click **Burn Tool** (🖐) in the list that appears.

● You can select the brush, the range of colors you want to affect, and the tool's exposure, or strength.

3 Click and drag over the area that you want to darken.

Photoshop darkens the area.

TIPS

How do I invert the bright and dark colors in an image?

Click **Image**, **Adjustments**, and then **Invert**. This makes the image look like a film negative. Bright colors become dark, and vice versa.

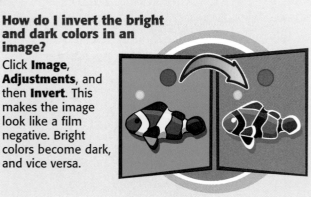

How can I add extra shadows to the bottom of an object?

Applying the **Burn** tool (🖐) with the Range set to Shadows offers a useful way to add shadows to the shaded side of an object. Likewise, you can use the **Dodge** tool (🔍) with the Range set to Highlights to add highlights to the lighter side of an object.

Using the Blur and Sharpen Tools

You can sharpen or blur specific areas of your image with the Sharpen and Blur tools. This enables you to emphasize or de-emphasize objects in a photo.

You can blur or sharpen the entire image by using one of the Blur or Sharpen commands located in Photoshop's Filter menu. See Chapter 10 for more information.

USING THE BLUR TOOL

1 Click the **Blur** tool (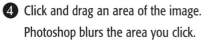).

2 Click the **Brush** ▯.

3 Select the brush that you want to use.

● To change the strength of the tool, type a value from **1%** to **100%**.

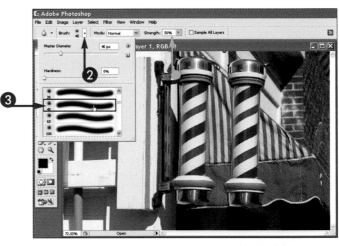

4 Click and drag an area of the image.

Photoshop blurs the area you click.

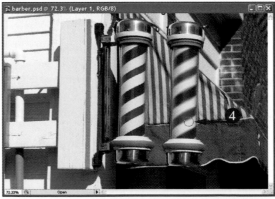

USING THE SHARPEN TOOL

1 Click and hold 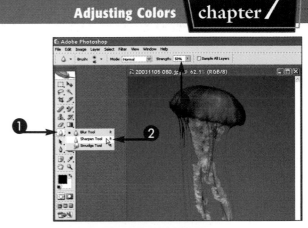.

2 Click **Sharpen Tool** (△) in the list that appears.

● You can type a value from **1%** to **100%** to set the strength of the tool.

3 Click and drag an area of the image.

Photoshop sharpens the area of the image you click.

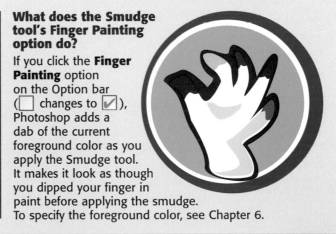

What is the Smudge tool?

The **Smudge** tool (🖐) simulates dragging a finger through wet paint, shifting colors and blurring your image. You can access it by clicking and holding the 🖐 tool.

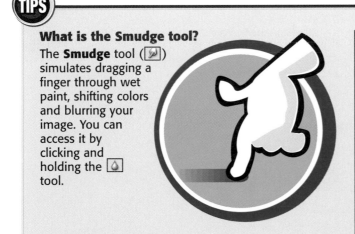

What does the Smudge tool's Finger Painting option do?

If you click the **Finger Painting** option on the Option bar (☐ changes to ☑), Photoshop adds a dab of the current foreground color as you apply the Smudge tool. It makes it look as though you dipped your finger in paint before applying the smudge. To specify the foreground color, see Chapter 6.

You can use the Levels command to make fine adjustments to the highlights, midtones, or shadows in an image.

Although more difficult to use, the Levels command offers more control over brightness than the Brightness/Contrast command, covered in the section "Change Brightness and Contrast."

To change only selected pixels, select them before performing the Levels command. Similarly, in a multilayered image, your adjustments affect only the selected layer.

Adjust Levels

① Click **Image**.

② Click **Adjustments**.

③ Click **Levels**.

The Levels dialog box appears.

④ To display your adjustments in the image window as you make them, click the **Preview** option (☐ changes to ☑).

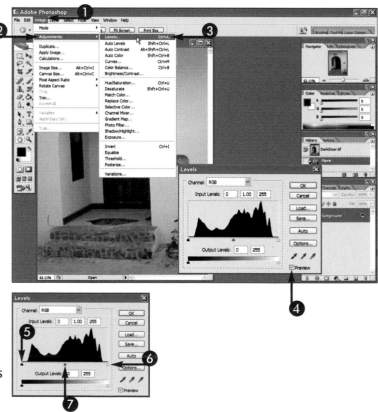

You can use the Input sliders to adjust an image's brightness, midtones, and highlights.

⑤ Click and drag ▲ to the right to darken shadows and increase contrast.

⑥ Click and drag △ to the left to lighten the bright areas of the image and increase contrast.

⑦ Click and drag ▲ to adjust the midtones of the image.

You can use the Output sliders to decrease the contrast while either lightening or darkening the image.

⑧ Click and drag ▣ to the right to lighten the image.

⑨ Click and drag ▢ to the left to darken the image.

⑩ Click **OK**.

Photoshop makes brightness and contrast adjustments to the image.

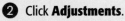

How do you adjust the brightness levels of an image automatically?

Use Photoshop's Auto Levels command. This converts the lightest pixels in the image to white and the darkest pixels in the image to black. This command is similar to the Auto Contrast command and can quickly improve the contrast of an overly gray photographic image. See the section "Change Brightness and Contrast" for more information.

❶ Click **Image**.

❷ Click **Adjustments**.

❸ Click **Auto Levels**.

Photoshop automatically adjusts the brightness levels in your image.

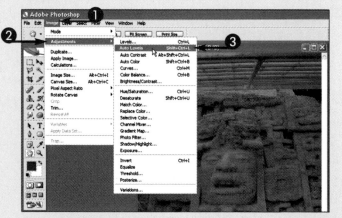

Adjust Hue and Saturation

You can change the hue to shift the component colors of an image. You can change the saturation to adjust the color intensity in an image.

If you make a selection before performing the Hue/Saturation command, you affect only the selected pixels. Similarly, if you have a multilayered image, your adjustments affect only the selected layer. See Chapter 4 to make a selection, and Chapter 8 for more about layers.

Adjust Hue and Saturation

① Click **Image**.

② Click **Adjustments**.

③ Click **Hue/Saturation**.

The Hue/Saturation dialog box appears.

④ To display your adjustments in the image window as you make them, click the **Preview** option (☐ changes to ☑).

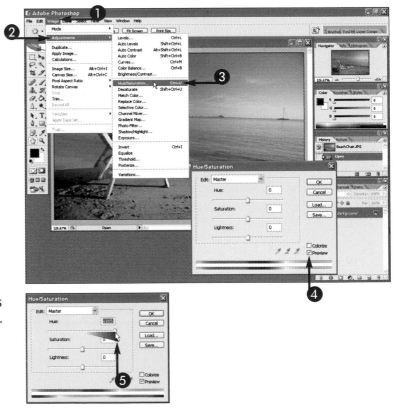

⑤ Click and drag the **Hue** slider (▣) to shift the colors in the image. See the tip on the next page for details.

Dragging ▣ left or right shifts the colors in different, and sometimes bizarre, ways.

6 Click and drag the **Saturation** slider (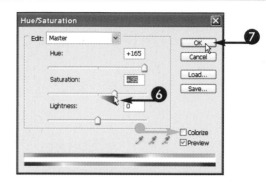).

Dragging 🔲 to the right or to the left increases or decreases the intensity of the image's colors, respectively.

● Clicking the **Colorize** option (☐ changes to ☑) turns the image into a monotone, or one-color, image. You can adjust the color with the sliders.

7 Click **OK**.

Photoshop makes the color adjustments to the image.

In this example, adjusting the hue has changed the blue ocean and sky to orange.

TIPS

How does Photoshop adjust an image's hues?

When you adjust an image's hues in Photoshop, its colors shift according to their position on the color wheel. The color wheel is a graphical way of presenting all the colors in the visible spectrum. Making a positive adjustment with the Hue slider shifts the colors in a counterclockwise direction; making a negative adjustment shifts the colors in a clockwise direction.

How can the Hue/Saturation command enhance my digital photos?

Boosting the saturation can improve photos that have colors that appear faded or washed out. Increasing the saturation by 10 to 20 points is often enough to enhance the colors without making them look artificially bright.

Using the Sponge Tool

You can use the Sponge tool to adjust the color saturation, or color intensity, of a specific area of an image. This can help bring out the colors in washed-out areas of photos, or mute colors in areas that are too bright.

Using the Sponge Tool

DECREASE SATURATION

1 Click and hold ⬚.

2 Click **Sponge Tool** (⬚) in the list that appears.

3 Click the **Brush** ⬚ and select the brush that you want to use.

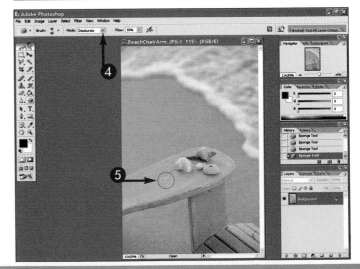

4 Click here and select **Desaturate**.

5 Click and drag the mouse (○) to decrease the saturation of an area of the image.

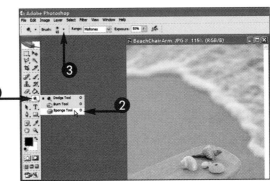

INCREASE SATURATION

1 Perform steps **1** to **3** on the previous page.

2 Click here and select **Saturate**.

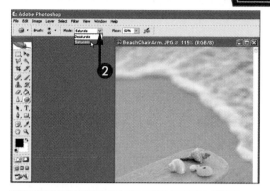

3 Click and drag ○ over that area of the image.

Photoshop increases the saturation of the area of the image.

● You can adjust the strength of the Sponge tool by typing a new Flow setting from **1%** to **100%**.

TIP

How can I easily convert a color image to a black-and-white image?

1 Click **Image**.

2 Click **Adjustments**.

3 Click **Desaturate**.

● Photoshop sets the saturation value of the image to 0, effectively converting it to a black-and-white image.

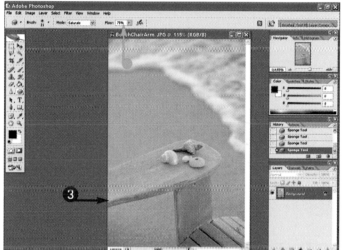

Adjust Color Balance

You can use the Color Balance command to change the amounts of specific colors in your image. This can be useful if you need to remove a color cast introduced by a scanner or by age.

If you make a selection before performing the Color Balance command, only the selected pixels are affected. Similarly, if you have a multilayered image, your adjustments affect only the selected layer. See Chapter 4 to make a selection and Chapter 8 for more about layers.

Adjust Color Balance

① Click **Image**.

② Click **Adjustments**.

③ Click **Color Balance**.

   The Color Balance dialog box appears.

④ To display your adjustments in the image window as you make them, click the **Preview** option (☐ changes to ☑).

⑤ Select the tones in the image that you want to affect (○ changes to ⊙).

⑥ Click and drag a color slider (▢) toward the color you want to add more of.

   To add a warm cast to your image, you can drag a slider toward red or magenta.

   To add a cool cast, you can drag a slider toward blue or cyan.

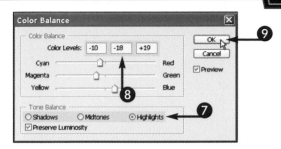

7 Select another Tone Balance option.

8 Type a number from **-100** to **100** in one or more of the color level fields.

Note: Step 8 is an alternative to dragging a slider.

9 Click **OK**.

Photoshop makes color adjustments to the image.

How can the Color Balance command help me improve poorly lit digital photos?

The Color Balance command can help eliminate a color cast that can sometimes permeate a digital photo. For example, some indoor incandescent or fluorescent lighting can add a yellowish or bluish tint to your images. You can remove these tints by adding blue or red, respectively, to your images using this command.

How can I convert my image to black-and-white pixels?

Click **Image**, **Adjustments**, and **Threshold**. The Bitmap dialog box appears, enabling you to choose a method for converting the pixels. This command makes your image look like a photocopy.

Using the Variations Command

The Variations command offers a user-friendly interface that enables you to adjust the color in your image.

If you make a selection before performing the Variations command, only the selected pixels are affected. Similarly, if you have a multilayered image, your adjustments affect only the selected layer. See Chapter 4 to make a selection, and Chapter 8 for more about layers.

Using the Variations Command

① Click **Image**.

② Click **Adjustments**.

③ Click **Variations**.

The Variations dialog box appears.

④ Select a tonal range of your image to adjust (○ changes to ◉).

● Alternatively, you can select **Saturation**, or strength of color (○ changes to ◉).

⑤ Click and drag 🔲 left to perform small adjustments, or right to make large adjustments.

⑥ To add a color to your image, click one of the **More** thumbnails.

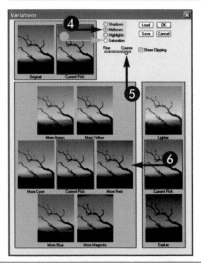

● The result of the adjustment appears in the Current Pick thumbnails.

  To increase the effect, you can click the **More** thumbnail again.

● You can decrease the brightness of the image by clicking **Darker**.

● You can increase the brightness by clicking **Lighter**.

⑦ Click **OK**.

  Photoshop makes the color adjustments to the image.

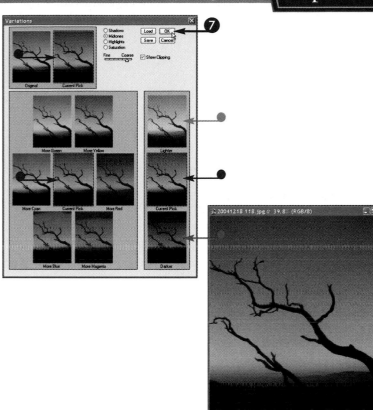

TIP

How can I undo color adjustments while using the Variations dialog box?

If you clicked one of the More thumbnail images to increase a color, you can click the **More** thumbnail image opposite to undo the effect.

When you add colors in equal amounts to an image, the colors opposite one another — for example, Green and Magenta — cancel each other out.

Note that clicking the **Original** image in the upper-left corner returns the image to its original state as well.

Match Colors between Images

You can use the Match Color command to match the colors in one image with the colors from another. For example, you can apply the colors from a bluish shoreline image to a reddish desert image to give the desert image a cooler appearance.

Match Colors between Images

1 Open a source image from which you want to match colors.

2 Open a destination image whose colors you want to change.

3 Click **Image**.

4 Click **Adjustments**.

5 Click **Match Color**.

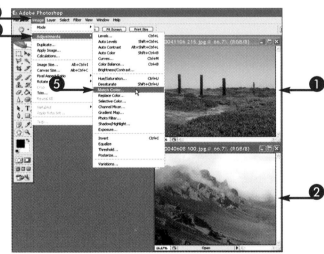

The Match Color dialog box opens.

6 Click here and select the file name of the source image.

7 Click and drag the sliders (▣) to control how the new colors are applied.

Luminance controls the brightness.

Color Intensity controls the saturation.

Fade controls how much color Photoshop replaces; you can increase the Fade value to greater than 0 to only partially replace the color.

8 Click **OK**.

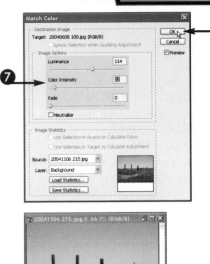

Photoshop replaces the colors in the destination image with those in the source image.

● In this example, Photoshop changes colors in a grayish crater scene to match a more red selection of colors from a beach scene.

TIP

How do I match colors using colors from only a selected part of my source image?
Make a selection before performing steps **3** to **5** in this section, and then click the **Use Selection in Source to Calculate Colors** option (○ changes to ◉) in the Match Color dialog box. Photoshop uses only colors from inside the selection to determine color replacement.

Correct Shadows and Highlights

You can quickly correct images with overly dark or light areas using the Shadow/Highlight command. This command can help correct photos that have a shadowed subject due to backlighting.

If you make a selection before performing the Shadow/Highlight command, only the selected pixels are affected. Similarly, if you have a multilayered image, your adjustments affect only the selected layer. See Chapter 4 to make a selection, and Chapter 8 for more about layers.

Correct Shadows and Highlights

① Click **Image**.

② Click **Adjustments**.

③ Click **Shadow/Highlight**.

The Shadow/Highlight dialog box appears.

④ Click and drag the **Shadows Amount** slider (⬚).

The further you drag the ⬚ to the right, the more the shadows lighten.

● You can also adjust the shadows by typing a number from **0** to **100**.

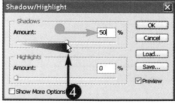

5 Click and drag the **Highlights Amount** slider ().

The further you drag the ⬚ to the right, the more the highlights darken.

● You can also adjust the highlights by typing a number from **0** to **100**.

6 Click **OK**.

Photoshop adjusts the shadows and highlights in the image.

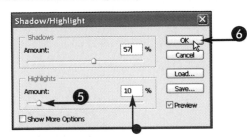

TIP

How do I get more control over how my shadows and highlights are affected by the Shadow/ Highlight command?

Click the **Show More Options** option (☐ changes to ☑) in the Shadow/Highlight dialog box. Additional settings appear. Adjusting the **Tonal Width** sliders help you control what parts of the image are considered shadows and highlights. The **Radius** sliders help you control the contrast in the adjusted shadows and highlights.

Create a Duotone

You can convert a grayscale image to a duotone. This is an easy way to add some color to a black-and-white photo.

A *duotone* is essentially a grayscale image with a color tint.

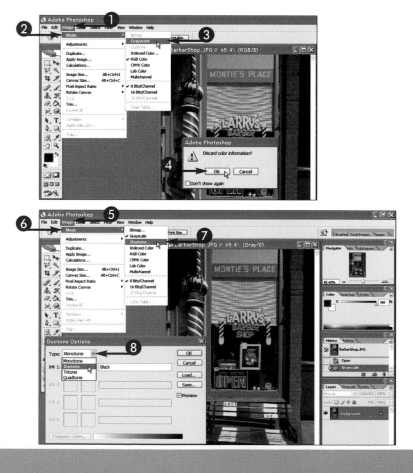

Create a Duotone

① Click **Image**.

② Click **Mode**.

③ Click **Grayscale**.

④ In the dialog box that appears, click **OK**.

Photoshop converts your image to grayscale.

⑤ Click **Image**.

⑥ Click **Mode**.

⑦ Click **Duotone**.

The Duotone Options dialog box opens.

⑧ Click here and select **Duotone**.

9 Click the first color swatch.

The Color Picker dialog box opens.

10 Click inside the window to select your first duotone color.

● You can click and drag the slider to change the color selection.

11 Click **OK**.

12 In the Duotone Options dialog box, type a name for the color.

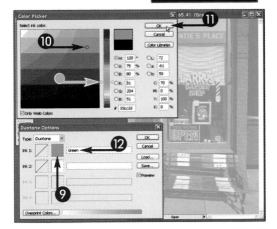

13 Click the second color swatch.

The Color Libraries dialog box opens.

14 Click inside the window to select your second duotone color.

15 Click **OK** in the Color Libraries dialog box.

16 Click **OK** in the Duotone Options dialog box.

Photoshop uses the two selected colors to create the tones in the image.

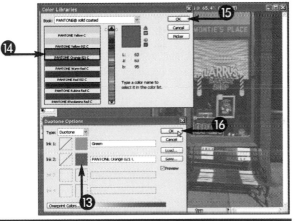

TIPS

How can I use duotones?

Duotones offer a quick and easy way to add color to a Web page or printed publication when all you have available are grayscale images.

Can I combine more than two colors to create the tones in my grayscale image?

Yes. You can combine three colors to create a tritone, or four colors to create a quadtone. Select **Tritone** or **Quadtone** instead of Duotone in the Type box in step **8** to create these types of images. You can also select **Monotone** to create your image tones using a single color.

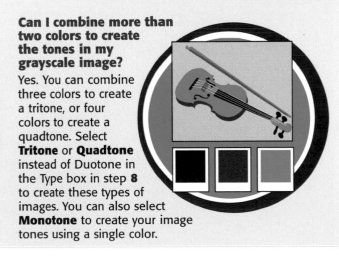

8

Working with Layers

Do you want to separate the elements in your image so that you can move and transform them independently of one another? You can do this by placing them in different layers.

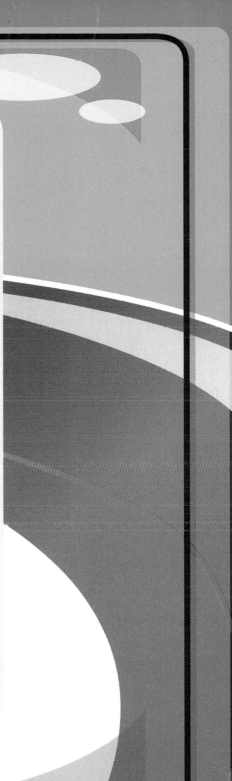

A Photoshop image can consist of multiple layers, with each layer containing different objects in the image.

Layer Independence

Layered Photoshop files act like several images combined into one. Each layer of an image has its own set of pixels that you can move and transform independently of the pixels in other layers.

Apply Commands to Layers

Most Photoshop commands affect only the layer that you select. For example, if you click and drag using the **Move** tool ( ), the selected layer moves while the other layers stay in place. If you apply a color adjustment, only colors in the selected layer change.

Manipulate Layers

You can combine, duplicate, and hide layers in an image. You can shuffle the order in which you stack layers. You can also link particular layers so that they move in unison.

Adjustment Layers

Adjustment layers are special layers that contain information about color or tonal adjustments. An adjustment layer affects the pixels in all the layers below it. You can increase or decrease an adjustment layer's intensity to get precisely the effect you want.

Transparency

Layers can have transparent areas, where the elements in the layers below can show through. When you perform a cut or erase command on a layer, the affected pixels become transparent.

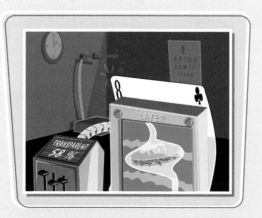

Save Layered Files

You can save multilayered images only in the Photoshop, PDF, and TIFF file formats. To save a layered image in another file format — for example, PICT, BMP, GIF, or JPEG — you must combine the image's layers into a single layer, a process known as *flattening*. For more information about saving files, see Chapter 14.

Create and Add to a Layer

To keep elements in your image independent of one another, you can create separate layers and add objects to them.

This example shows adding content to the new layer by copying and pasting from another image file.

CREATE A LAYER

① Click the **Layers** tab to select the Layers palette.

   If the Layers tab is hidden, you can click **Window** and then **Layers** to open the Layers palette.

② Click the layer above which you want to add the new layer.

③ In the Layers palette, click the **New Layer** button (⬜).

   Alternatively, you can click **Layer**, **New**, and then **Layer**.

● Photoshop creates a new, transparent layer.

Note: To change the name of a layer, see the section "Rename a Layer."

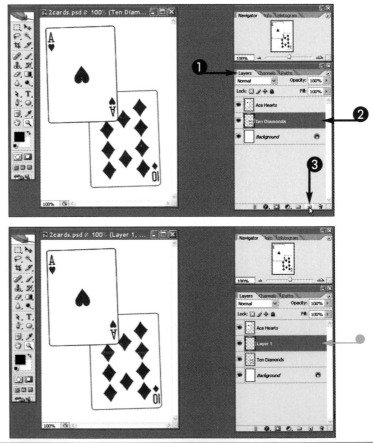

COPY AND PASTE INTO A LAYER

1. Open another image.

2. Using a selection tool, select the content you want to copy into the other image.

Note: See Chapter 1 for more about opening an image. See Chapter 4 for more about the selection tools.

3. Click **Edit**.

4. Click **Copy**.

5. Click the image window where you created the new layer.

6. Click the new layer in the Layers palette.

7. Click **Edit**.

8. Click **Paste**.

● The selected content from the other image appears in the new layer.

TIP

What is the Background layer?

The Background layer is the default bottom layer that appears when you create a new image that has a nontransparent background color, or when you import an image from a scanner or digital camera. You can create new layers on top of a Background layer, but not below it. Unlike other layers, a Background layer cannot contain transparent pixels.

Hide a Layer

You can hide a layer to temporarily remove elements in that layer from view.

Hidden layers do not display when you print or use the Save for Web command.

Hide a Layer

❶ Click the **Layers** tab to select the Layers palette.

If the Layers tab is hidden, you can click **Window** and then **Layers** to open the Layers palette.

❷ Click a layer.

❸ Click the **Eye** icon (👁) for the layer.

The icon disappears.

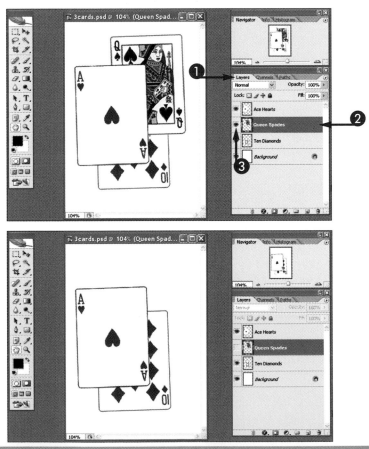

Photoshop hides the layer.

To show one layer and hide all the others, you can press <kbd>Alt</kbd> (<kbd>Option</kbd> on the Mac) and click the 👁 for the layer you want to show.

Note: *You can also delete a layer. See the section "Delete a Layer" for more information.*

Move a Layer

You can use the Move tool to reposition the elements in one layer without moving those in others.

Move a Layer

① Click the **Layers** tab to select the Layers palette.

If the Layers tab is hidden, you can click **Window** and then **Layers** to open the Layers palette.

② Click a layer.

③ Click the **Move** tool (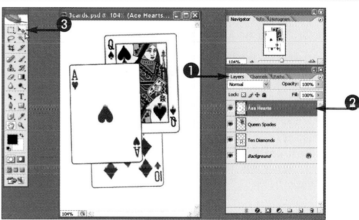).

④ Click and drag inside the window.

Content in the selected layer moves.

Content in the other layers does not move.

Note: To move several layers at the same time, see the section "Link Layers."

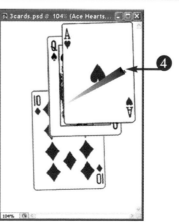

Duplicate a Layer

By duplicating a layer, you can manipulate elements in an image while keeping a copy of their original state.

Duplicate a Layer

① Click the **Layers** tab to select the Layers palette.

If the Layers tab is hidden, you can click **Window** and then **Layers** to open the Layers palette.

② Click a layer.

③ Click and drag the layer to ⬛.

Alternatively, you can click **Layer** and then **Duplicate Layer**, in which case a dialog box appears, asking you to name the layer you want to duplicate.

● Photoshop duplicates the selected layer.

Note: To rename the duplicate layer, see the section "Rename a Layer."

● You can see that Photoshop has duplicated the layer by selecting the new layer, clicking ▣, and clicking and dragging the layer.

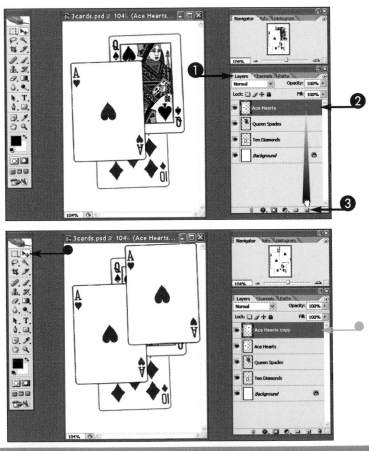

Delete a Layer

You can delete a layer when you no longer have a use for its contents.

Delete a Layer

1 Click the **Layers** tab to select the Layers palette.

2 Click a layer.

3 Click and drag the layer to the **Trash** icon (🗑).

Alternatively, you can click **Layer** and then **Delete Layer**, or you can select a layer and click 🗑. In both cases, a confirmation dialog box appears.

Photoshop deletes the selected layer, and the content in the layer disappears from the image window.

Note: You can also hide a layer. See the section "Hide a Layer" for more information.

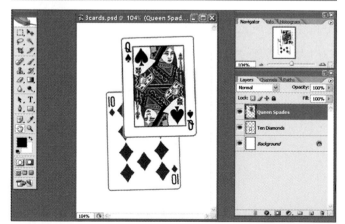

Reorder Layers

You can change the stacking order of layers to move elements forward or backward in your image.

USING THE LAYERS PALETTE

1 Click the **Layers** tab to select the Layers palette.

If the Layers tab is hidden, you can click **Window** and then **Layers** to open the palette.

2 Click a layer.

3 Click and drag the layer to change its arrangement in the stack.

● The layer assumes its new position in the stack.

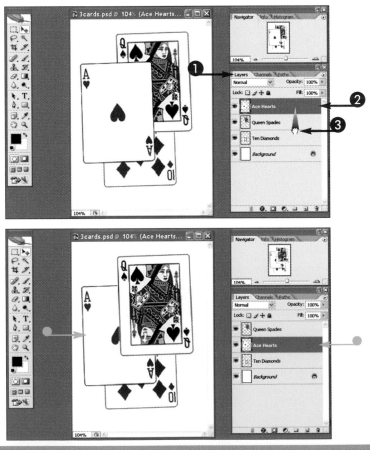

USING THE ARRANGE COMMANDS

1 Click a layer.

2 Click **Layer**.

3 Click **Arrange**.

4 Click the command for how you want to move the layer: **Bring to Front**, **Bring Forward**, **Send Backward**, **Send to Back**, or **Reverse**.

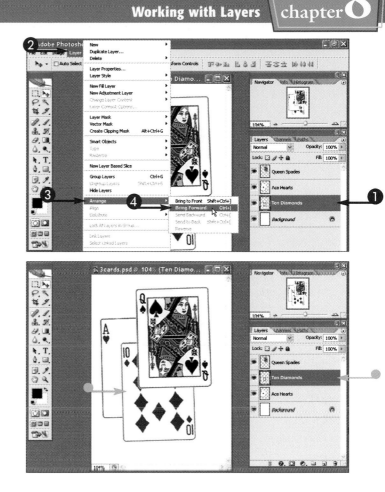

● The layer assumes its new position in the stack.

Note: You cannot move a layer in back of the default Background layer.

Are there shortcuts for changing the order of layers?
You can shift layers forward and backward in the stack by pressing the following shortcuts keys:

Move...	Windows Shortcut	Mac Shortcut
...forward one step	Ctrl +]	⌘ +]
...backward	Ctrl + [	⌘ + [
...to the very front	Shift + Ctrl +]	Shift + ⌘ +]
...to the very back	Shift + Ctrl + [	Shift + ⌘ + [

Change the Opacity of a Layer

Adjusting the opacity of a layer can let elements in the layers below show through. *Opacity* is the opposite of transparency. Decreasing the opacity of a layer increases its transparency.

Change the Opacity of a Layer

① Click the **Layers** tab to select the Layers palette.

If the Layers tab is hidden, you can click **Window** and then **Layers** to open the Layers palette.

② Click a layer other than the Background layer.

Note: You cannot change the opacity of the Background layer.

The default opacity is 100%, which is completely opaque.

③ Type a new value in the **Opacity** field and press Enter (Return on a Mac).

● Alternatively, you can click ▶ and drag the slider.

A layer's opacity can range from 0% to 100%.

● The layer changes in opacity.

A shortcut for changing layer opacity is to click the layer and type a number key.

● In this example, **3** was typed, which changes the opacity to 30%.

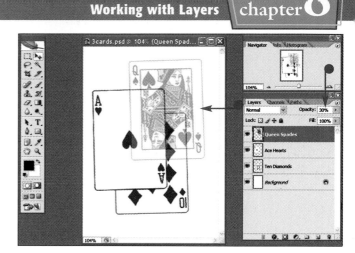

You can make multiple layers in your image semitransparent by changing their opacities.

● In this example, both the Queen of Spades and Ten of Diamonds layers are semitransparent.

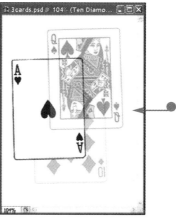

TIP

What is the Fill setting in the Layers palette?

It is similar to the opacity setting, except that lowering it does not affect any blending options or layer styles applied to the layer. For example, if you applied a drop shadow to a layer, lowering the Fill makes the layer object more transparent but does not affect the shadow behind the object. Lowering the Opacity *does* affect blending options and layer styles. For more about blending options, see the section "Blend Layers." For more about layer styles, see Chapter 9.

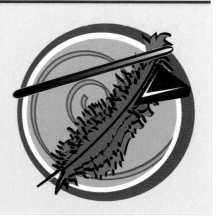

Merge and Flatten Layers

Merging layers enables you to permanently combine information from two or more separate layers. Flattening layers combines all the layers of an image into one.

MERGE LAYERS

1 Click the **Layers** tab to select the Layers palette.

If the Layers tab is hidden, you can click **Window** and then **Layers** to open the Layers palette.

2 Place the two layers you want to merge next to each other.

Note: See the section "Reorder Layers" to change the stacking order.

3 Click the topmost of the two layers.

4 Click **Layer**.

5 Click **Merge Down**.

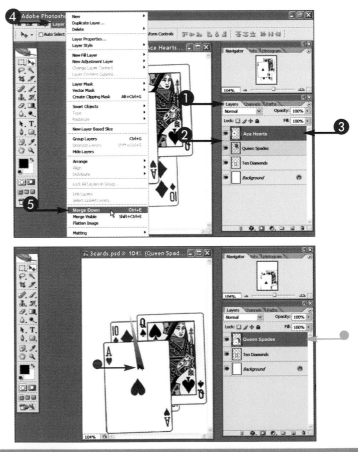

● The two layers merge.

Photoshop keeps the name of the lower layer.

● To see the result of the merge, select the new layer, click ▶⊕, and click and drag the merged layer; the elements that were previously in separate layers now move together.

FLATTEN LAYERS

1 Click **Layer**.

2 Click **Flatten Image**.

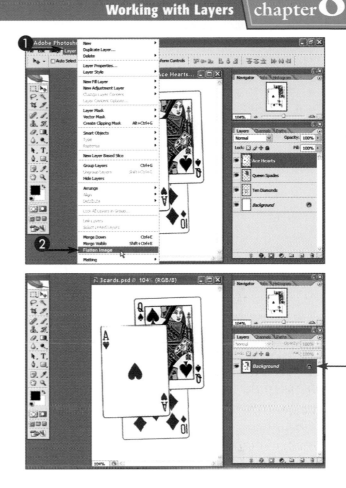

● All the layers merge into one.

TIP

Why would I want to merge layers?

Merging layers enables you to save computer memory. The fewer layers a Photoshop image has, the less space it takes up in RAM and on your hard drive when you save it. Merging layers also lets you permanently combine elements of your image when you are happy with how you have arranged them relative to one another. If you want the option of rearranging all the original layers in the future, save a copy of your image before you merge layers.

Rename a Layer

You can rename a layer to give it a name that describes its content.

Rename a Layer

1. Click the **Layers** tab to select the Layers palette.

   If the Layers tab is hidden, you can click **Window** and then **Layers** to open the Layers palette.

2. Click a layer.

3. Click **Layer**.

4. Click **Layer Properties**.

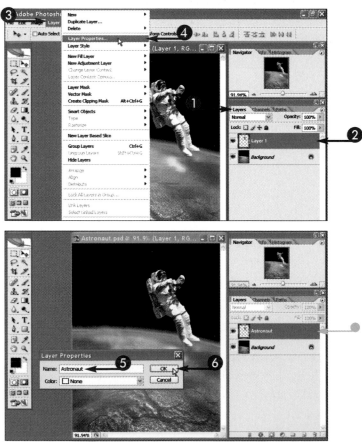

The Layer Properties dialog box appears.

5. Type a new name for the layer.

6. Click **OK**.

● The name of the layer changes in the Layers palette.

   You can also double-click the name of the layer in the Layers palette to edit the name in place.

You can use a transform tool to change the shape of the objects in a layer. When you transform a layer, the rest of your image remains unchanged.

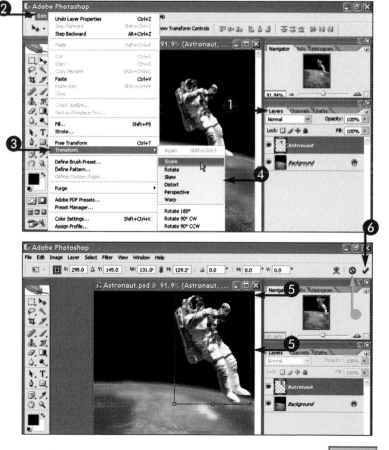

Transform a Layer

① Click the **Layers** tab to select the Layers palette.

If the Layers tab is hidden, you can click **Window** and then **Layers** to open the Layers palette.

② Click **Edit**.

③ Click **Transform**.

④ Click a transform command.

⑤ Click and drag the side and corner handles to transform the shape of the layer.

⑥ Click ✔ or press Enter (Return) to apply the change.

● You can click ⊘ or press Esc (⌘+ . on a Mac) to cancel the change.

Photoshop changes your image according to the transform command you selected.

Note: *For more about transforming your images, see Chapter 5.*

Create a Solid Fill Layer

You can create a solid fill layer to place an opaque layer of color throughout your image.

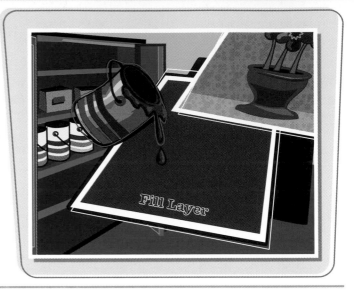

Create a Solid Fill Layer

① Click the **Layers** tab to select the Layers palette.

If the Layers tab is hidden, you can click **Window** and then **Layers** to open the Layers palette.

② Click the layer above which you want to add solid color.

③ Click **Layer**.

④ Click **New Fill Layer**.

⑤ Click **Solid Color**.

● You can also click the **Create new fill or adjustment layer** button (●) and select **Solid Color**.

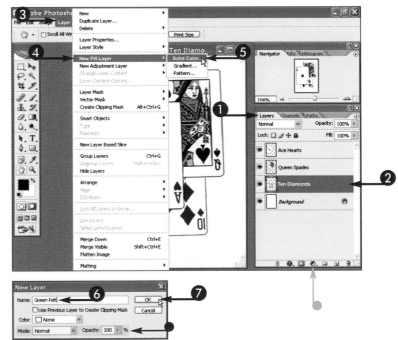

The New Layer dialog box appears.

⑥ Type a name for the layer.

● You can specify a blend mode or opacity setting for the layer.

Note: See the section "Blend Layers" or "Change the Opacity of a Layer" for details.

⑦ Click **OK**.

The Color Picker dialog box appears.

8 To change the range of colors that appears in the window, click and drag the slider (▷).

9 To select a fill color, click in the color window.

10 Click **OK**.

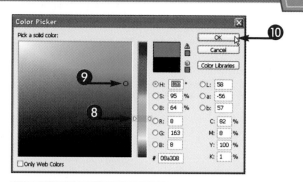

● Photoshop creates a new layer filled with a solid color.

Layers above the new layer are not affected.

TIP

How do I add solid color to just part of a layer?

Make a selection with a selection tool before creating the solid fill layer. Photoshop adds color only inside the selection.

You can create a gradient fill layer to place a color transition throughout your image.

For another way to add a gradient to your image, see Chapter 6.

Create a Gradient Fill Layer

① Click the **Layers** tab to select the Layers palette.

If the Layers tab is hidden, you can click **Window** and then **Layers** to open the Layers palette.

② Click the layer above which you want to add a pattern.

③ Click **Layer**.

④ Click **New Fill Layer**.

⑤ Click **Gradient**.

● You can also click 🖉 and select **Gradient**.

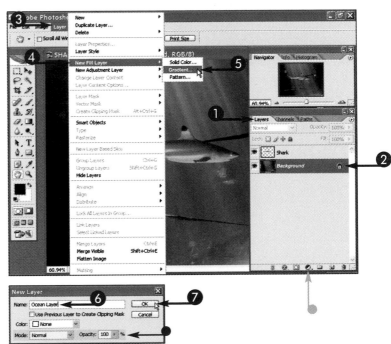

The New Layer dialog box appears.

⑥ Type a name for the layer.

● You can specify a blend mode or opacity setting for the layer.

Note: *See the section "Blend Layers" or "Change the Opacity of a Layer" for details.*

⑦ Click **OK**.

The Gradient Fill dialog box appears.

8 Click here and select a set of gradient colors from the menu that appears.

9 Select your other gradient settings.

You can select a style to specify the shape.

You can select an angle to specify the direction.

10 Click **OK**.

● Photoshop creates a new layer filled with the specified gradient.

Layers above the new layer remain unaffected.

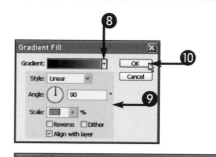

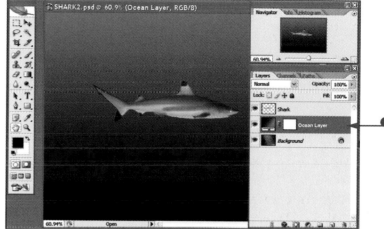

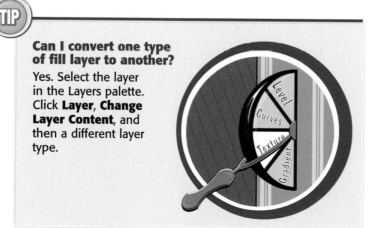

TIP

Can I convert one type of fill layer to another?

Yes. Select the layer in the Layers palette. Click **Layer**, **Change Layer Content**, and then a different layer type.

Create an Adjustment Layer

Adjustment layers let you store color and tonal changes in a layer, rather than having them permanently applied to your image.

Create an Adjustment Layer

① Click the **Layers** tab to select the Layers palette.

If the Layers tab is hidden, you can click **Window** and then **Layers** to open the Layers palette.

② Click a layer.

③ Click **Layer**.

④ Click **New Adjustment Layer**.

⑤ Click an adjustment command.

● You can also click ◯. and select an adjustment command.

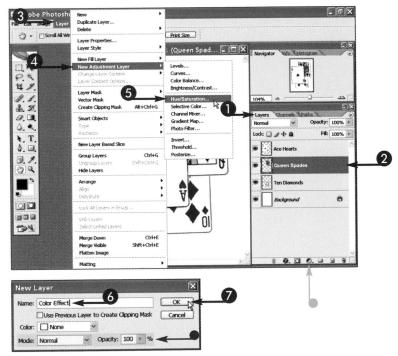

The New Layer dialog box appears.

⑥ Type a name for the adjustment layer.

● You can specify a blend mode or opacity setting for the layer.

Note: See the section "Blend Layers" or "Change the Opacity of a Layer" for details.

⑦ Click **OK**.

Photoshop places the new adjustment layer above the currently selected layer.

The dialog box for the adjustment command appears.

8 Click and drag the sliders (☐) or type values to adjust the settings.

In this example, an adjustment layer is created that changes the hue and saturation of the image.

9 Click **OK**.

● Photoshop creates an adjustment layer.

Photoshop applies the effect to the layers below the adjustment layer, including the background layer.

● In this example, the adjustment layer affects the card layers below it while leaving the card layer above it unaffected.

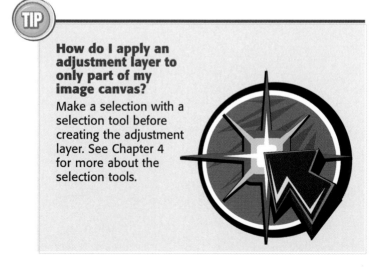

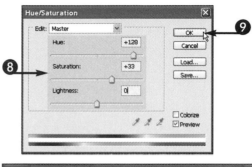

TIP

How do I apply an adjustment layer to only part of my image canvas?

Make a selection with a selection tool before creating the adjustment layer. See Chapter 4 for more about the selection tools.

Edit an
Adjustment Layer

You can modify the color and
tonal changes that you defined
in an adjustment layer. This
enables you to fine-tune your
adjustment layer to get the effect
you want.

Edit an Adjustment Layer

1 Click the **Layers** tab to select the Layers
palette.

If the Layers tab is hidden, you can click
Window and then **Layers** to open the
Layers palette.

2 Double-click the Adjustment layer's icon
in the Layers palette.

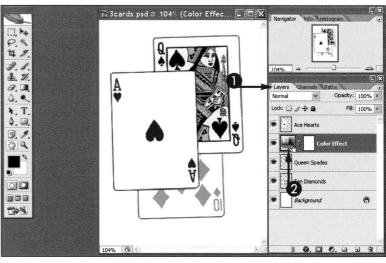

The settings dialog box corresponding to
the adjustment command appears.

3 Click and drag the sliders (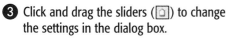) to change
the settings in the dialog box.

4 Click **OK**.

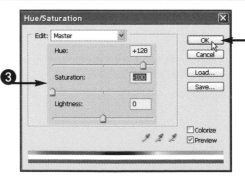

Photoshop applies your changes.

In this example, the saturation was reduced to the minimum, which removed the color in the layers below the adjustment layer.

● You can lessen the effect of an adjustment layer by decreasing the layer's opacity to less than 100%.

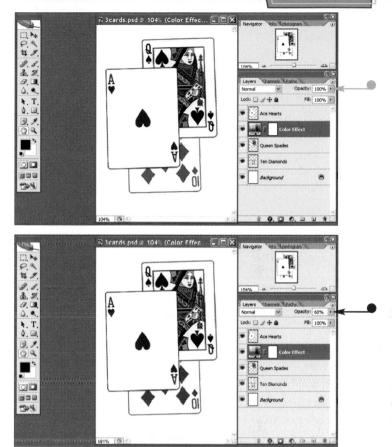

● In this example, the opacity was decreased to 60%, which reverses the decrease in saturation. Some of the original color in the cards returns.

TIP

How do I merge an adjustment layer with a regular layer?

Place the adjustment layer over the layer with which you want to merge it and then click **Layer** and **Merge Down**. When you merge the layers, Photoshop applies the adjustment layer's effects only to the layer with which it merged. The other layers below it remain unaffected. However, after you merge an adjustment layer, you can no longer edit its effects.

Linking causes multiple layers to move in unison when you rearrange them with the Move tool. You may find linking useful when you want to keep elements of an image aligned with one another, but do not want to merge their layers. See the section "Merge and Flatten Layers" for more about merging. Keeping layers unmerged enables you to apply effects independently to each one.

Link Layers

CREATE A LINK

① Click the **Layers** tab to select the Layers palette.

If the Layers tab is hidden, you can click **Window** and then **Layers** to open the Layers palette.

② Press Ctrl (⌘ on a Mac).

③ Click the layers you want to link.

④ Click **Layer**.

⑤ Click **Link Layers**.

● Doing so turns on a linking icon (🔗).

The layers link together.

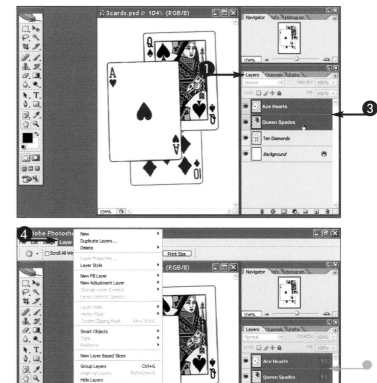

MOVE LINKED LAYERS

1 Click 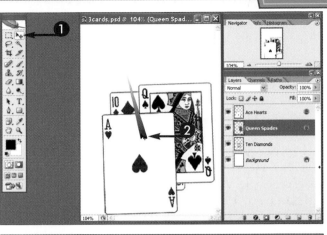.

2 Click and drag inside the image window.

The linked layers move together.

You can link as many nonbackground layers as you want.

You cannot link the Background layer with other layers.

● In this example, all the nonbackground layers have been linked.

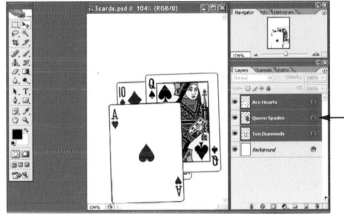

TIP

How do I keep from changing a layer after I have it the way I want it?

You can lock the layer by selecting the layer and clicking the **Lock** icon (🔒) in the Layers palette. You cannot move, delete, or otherwise edit a locked layer. You click the **lock transparency pixel** icon (▨) to prevent a user from editing the transparent pixels in the layer. Clicking the **lock image pixel** icon, which looks like a paintbrush (🖌), locks the nontransparent pixels in a layer, while clicking the **lock position** icon (✛) locks the position of a layer.

Blend Layers

You can use Photoshop's blending modes to specify how pixels in a layer blend with the layers below it.

BLEND A REGULAR LAYER

① Click the **Layers** tab to select the Layers palette.

If the Layers tab is hidden, you can click **Window** and then **Layers** to open the Layers palette.

② Click the layer that you want to blend.

③ Click here and select a blend mode.

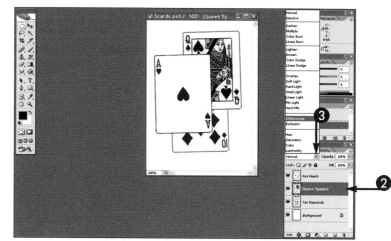

Photoshop blends the selected layer with the layers below it.

This example shows the Difference mode, which creates a photo-negative effect where the selected layer overlaps other layers including the Background layer.

BLEND AN ADJUSTMENT LAYER

1️⃣ Click the **Layers** tab to select the Layers palette.

If the Layers tab is hidden, you can click **Window** and then **Layers** to open the Layers palette.

2️⃣ Click an adjustment layer that you want to blend.

3️⃣ Click here and select a blend mode.

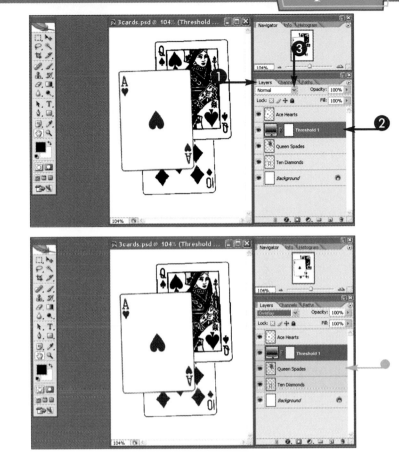

● Photoshop blends the selected layer with the layers below it.

This example shows the Overlay mode applied to a Threshold adjustment layer, which lets some of the original color through.

TIP

What effects do some of the different blending modes have?

The Multiply mode darkens the colors where the selected layer overlaps layers below it. The Screen mode is the opposite of Multiply: It lightens colors where layers overlap. Color takes the selected layer's colors and blends them with the details in the layers below it. Luminosity is the opposite of Color: It takes the selected layer's details and mixes them with the colors below it.

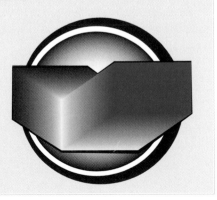

Work with Smart Objects

You can convert a layer into a smart object. Smart objects can be duplicated in your image, just like layers. But unlike regular layers, when you edit one copy of a smart object, all the copies of the smart object in your image are updated.

CREATE A SMART OBJECT

1 Click the layer to convert into a smart object.

2 Click **Layer**.

3 Click **Smart Objects**.

4 Click **Group into New Smart Object**.

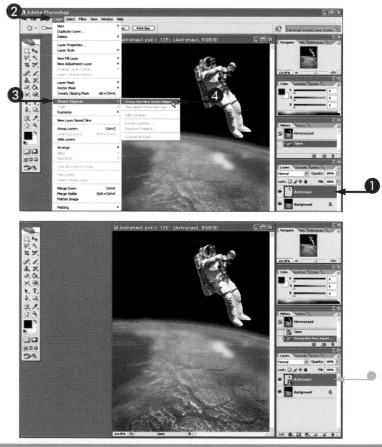

● Photoshop converts the layer into a smart object.

Smart objects are designated with a special icon (⬛) in the Layers palette.

DUPLICATE A SMART OBJECT

1 Click a smart object in the Layers palette.

2 Click **Layer**.

3 Click **Smart Objects**.

4 Click **New Smart Object via Copy**.

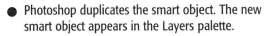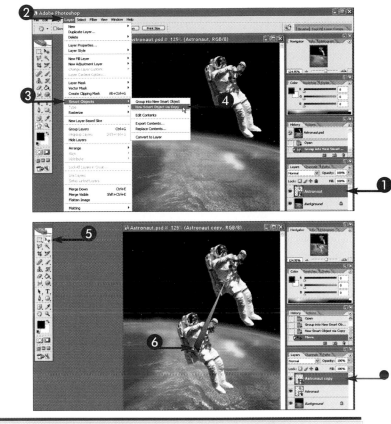

● Photoshop duplicates the smart object. The new smart object appears in the Layers palette.

5 Click ▶✛.

6 Click and drag to view the new smart object.

continued ➜

TIP

How do I convert a smart object back to a layer?

1 Click the smart object in the Layers palette.

2 Click **Layer**.

3 Click **Smart Objects**.

4 Click **Convert to Layer**.

Photoshop converts the smart object back to a layer.

When you edit a smart object, Photoshop opens it in its own window. After editing, you can save the changes and close the window. Photoshop then updates the smart object in your image as well as any of its copies.

Work with Smart Objects *(continued)*

EDIT A SMART OBJECT

① Click to select the smart object in the Layers palette.

② Click **Layer**.

③ Click **Smart Objects**.

④ Click **Edit Contents**.

A dialog box appears with editing details.

⑤ Click **OK**.

- Photoshop opens the smart object in a new window.

⑥ Edit your smart object.

In this example, color is applied to the smart object with the **Paintbrush** tool (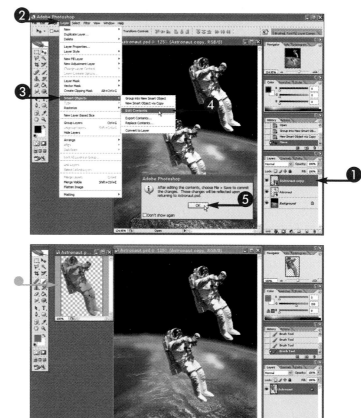).

190

7 Click **File**.

8 Click **Save**.

Photoshop saves the changes to the smart object.

9 Click the **Close** button (⊠) .

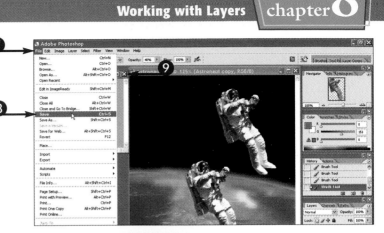

Photoshop closes the smart object.

● Photoshop updates the smart objects and any of its copies in the image.

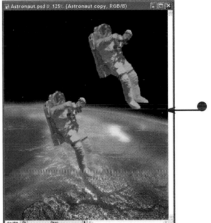

TIP

How can I insert another image into my image as a smart object?

You can use the Place command to insert a separate image as a smart object:

1 Click **File**.

2 Click **Place**.

The Place dialog box appears.

3 Click your image's filename.

4 Click **Place**.

5 Press **Enter** (**Return**) to complete the Place command.

Photoshop adds the image as a smart object.

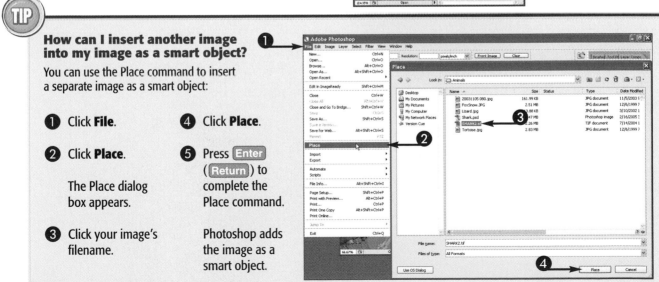

Applying Layer Styles

You can add special effects to layers by applying Photoshop's built-in layer styles. With these styles, you can add shadows, glows, and 3-D appearances to your layers. Photoshop's Styles palette enables you to easily apply predefined combinations of styles to your image and save your own styles for later use.

Apply a Drop Shadow

You can apply a drop shadow to make a layer look as though it is raised off the image canvas.

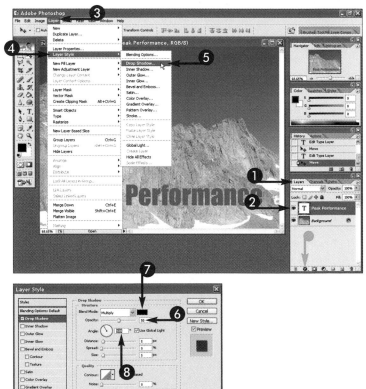

Apply a Drop Shadow

1. Click the **Layers** tab to select the Layers palette.
2. Click the layer to which you want to add the effect.
3. Click **Layer**.
4. Click **Layer Style**.
5. Click **Drop Shadow**.

● You can also click the **Add a layer style** button ( ) and select **Drop Shadow**.

The Layer Style dialog box opens.

Note: *Perform steps 6 to 11 if you want to enter your own settings. If you want to use the default settings, you can skip to step 12.*

6. Type an Opacity value to specify the shadow's transparency.
7. Click the color swatch to select a shadow color.

Note: *The default shadow color is black.*

8. Type an Angle value to specify in which direction the shadow is displaced.

⑨ Type a Distance value to specify how far the shadow is displaced.

⑩ Type a Spread value to specify the fuzziness of the shadow's edge.

⑪ Type a Size value to specify the size of the shadow's edge.

⑫ Click **OK**.

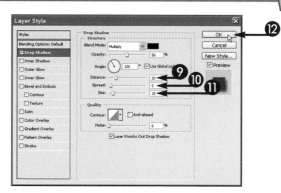

● Photoshop creates a shadow in back of the selected layer.

⑬ Click in the Layers palette (changes to).

● Photoshop displays the name of the style and the effects employed.

Note: In this example, the effect was applied to a text layer. For more information about text, see Chapter 12.

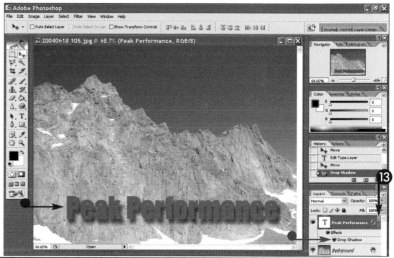

TIP

How do I add an inner shadow to a layer?

An inner shadow creates a cutout effect, with the selected layer appearing to drop behind the image canvas. To apply it:

① Click a layer in the Layers palette.

② Click **Layer**.

③ Click **Layer Style**.

④ Click **Inner Shadow**.

● Photoshop applies the style to objects in the layer.

Apply an
Outer Glow

The Outer Glow effect adds
faint coloring to the outside
edge of a layer.

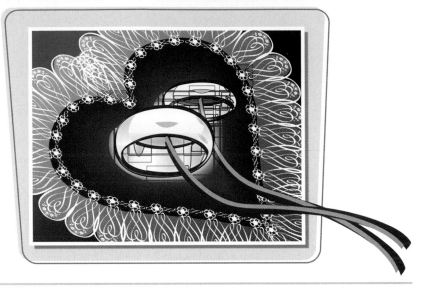

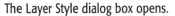

1 Click the **Layers** tab to select the Layers palette.

2 Click the layer to which you want to add the style.

3 Click **Layer**.

4 Click **Layer Style**.

5 Click **Outer Glow**.

● You can also click 🔲 and select **Outer Glow**.

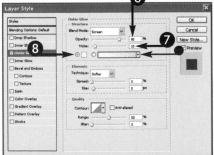

The Layer Style dialog box opens.

Note: *Perform steps 6 to 10 if you want to enter your own Outer Glow settings. If you want to use the default settings, you can skip to step 11.*

6 Type an Opacity value to specify the glow's darkness.

7 Specify a Noise value to add speckling to the glow.

8 Click the color swatch to choose the color of the glow (○ changes to ◉).

● You can also select from a series of preset color gradients by clicking ⬝.

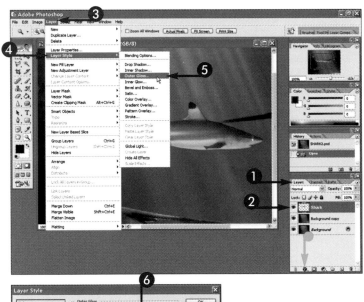

⑨ Type a Spread value to determine the fuzziness of the glow.

⑩ Type a Size value to specify the size of the glow.

⑪ Click **OK**.

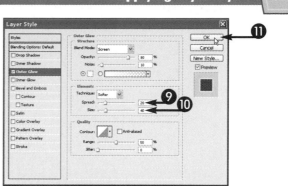

● Photoshop creates a glow around the outer edge of the selected layer.

⑫ Click ▌ in the Layers palette (▌ changes to ▌).

● Photoshop displays the name of the style and the effects employed.

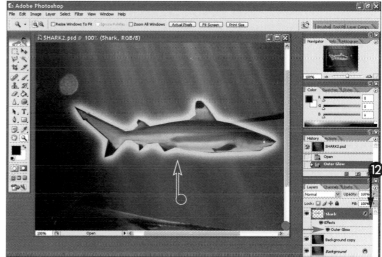

TIP

How do I give elements in a layer an inner glow?

An Inner Glow style adds color to the inside edge of a layer's object. To apply it:

❶ Click a layer in the Layers palette.

❷ Click **Layer**.

❸ Click **Layer Style**.

❹ Click **Inner Glow**.

● Photoshop applies the style to objects in the layer.

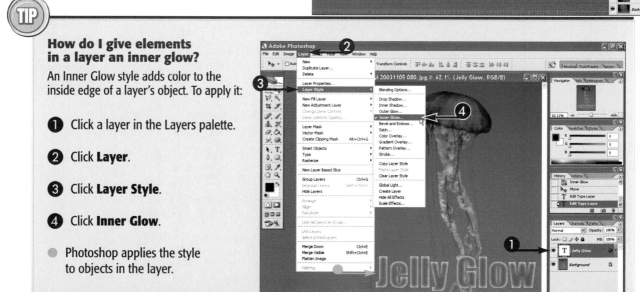

Apply Beveling and Embossing

You can bevel and emboss a layer to give it a three-dimensional look. This can make objects in the layer stand out and seem to rise off the screen.

① Click the **Layers** tab to select the Layers palette.

② Click the layer to which you want to add the style.

③ Click **Layer**.

④ Click **Layer Style**.

⑤ Click **Bevel and Emboss**.

● You can also click and select **Bevel and Emboss**.

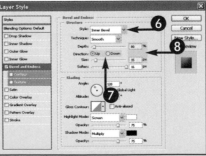

The Layer Style dialog box opens.

Note: *Perform steps **6** to **9** if you want to enter your own settings. If you want to use the default settings, you can skip to step **10**.*

⑥ Select an effect style.

Clicking **Inner Bevel** creates a three-dimensional look.

⑦ Specify the direction of the style's shadowing (○ changes to ⊙).

⑧ Type Depth and Size values to control the magnitude of the style.

⑨ Specify the direction of the shading with the Angle and Altitude values.

● You can click 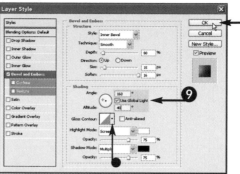 and select one of the Gloss Contour settings to apply abstract styles to your layer.

⑩ Click **OK**.

● Photoshop applies the Bevel and Emboss settings to the layer.

⑪ Click ▮ in the Layers palette (▮ changes to ▮).

● Photoshop displays the name of the style and the effects employed.

Note: *In this example, the style was applied to a text layer. For more about text, see Chapter 12.*

When would I use the Bevel and Emboss style?

The style can be useful for creating three-dimensional buttons for Web pages or multimedia applications. For example, to create a 3-D button, you can apply Bevel and Emboss to a colored rectangle and then add type over it.

How else can I enhance the 3-D effect of Bevel and Emboss?

You can click the **Contour** option (☐ changes to ☑) in the left-hand column of the Layer Style dialog box to darken the shading, or click the **Texture** option (☐ changes to ☑) to add shadowing that is slightly wavy.

Apply Multiple Styles to a Layer

You can apply multiple styles to layers in your image. This enables you to enhance the look of your layers in complex ways.

Apply Multiple Styles to a Layer

APPLY THE FIRST STYLE

1. Click the **Layers** tab.

● If the Layers tab is hidden, you can click **Window** and then **Layers**.

In this example, Gradient Overlay and Bevel and Emboss styles are applied.

2. Click **Layer**.
3. Click **Layer Style**.
4. Click the name of the first style that you want to apply.

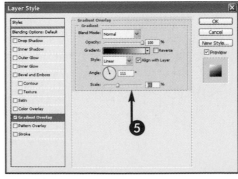

The Layer Style dialog box opens.

5. Specify the settings for the first style.

In this example, a Gradient Overlay is applied to the layer.

APPLY THE SECOND STYLE

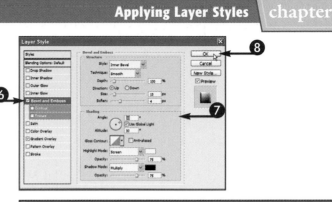

⑥ Click the name of the next style you want to apply.

⑦ Specify the settings for this style.

In this example, the Bevel and Emboss style is also applied to the layer.

You can apply other styles to the layer by repeating steps **6** and **7**.

⑧ Click **OK**.

● Photoshop applies the styles to the layer.

⑨ Click ▮ in the Layers palette (▮ changes to ▮).

● The effects appear below the selected layer in the Layers palette.

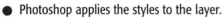

TIPS

How do I turn off layer effects that I have applied?

When you apply a style to a layer, Photoshop adds the style to the Layers palette. You may have to click ▮ to see a layer's effects (▮ changes to ▮). You can temporarily turn off an effect by clicking the **Eye** icon (👁) in the Layers palette. You can turn the effect on by clicking the now-empty box again to make 👁 reappear.

Is there a quick way to remove the styles from a layer?

Select the layer and click **Layer**, **Layer Style**, and **Clear Layer Style**. Photoshop removes all the styles currently applied to the layer.

Edit a Layer Style

You can edit a layer style that you have applied to your image. This enables you to fine-tune the effect to achieve an appearance that suits you.

① Click the **Layers** tab.

If the Layers tab is hidden, you can click **Window** and then **Layers**.

In this example, the color overlay of a layer object is edited.

② Click **Layer**.

③ Click **Layer Style**.

④ Click the style you want to edit.

You can also double-click the style's name in the Layers palette.

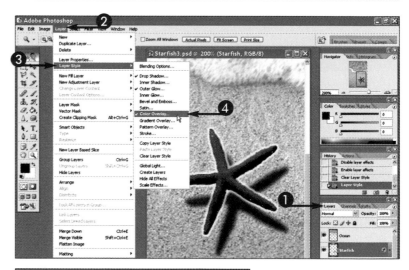

The Layer Style dialog box opens.

● Photoshop displays the current configuration values for the style.

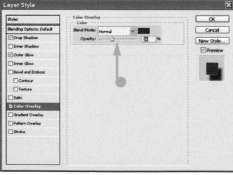

⑤ Edit the values in the Layer Style dialog box.

This example changes a color overlay.

⑥ Click **OK**.

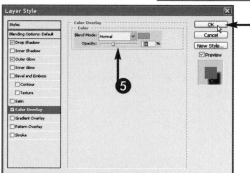

● Photoshop applies the edited style to the layer.

You can edit a style as many times as you want.

TIPS

How do I keep a layer effect from accidentally being changed?

You can lock a layer and its styles by selecting the layer and clicking the **Lock** icon (🔒) in the Layers palette; the button depresses and becomes highlighted. The layer is then locked, which means that you cannot change its styles or apply any more Photoshop commands to it. You can also click the **Lock Transparent Pixels** icon (▣), the **Lock Image Pixels** icon (✏), or the **Lock Position** icon (✛) to lock a layer's transparent pixels, its nontransparent pixels, or its position, respectively.

Can I copy styles between layers?

Yes. Select the layer you want to copy from, then click **Layer**, **Layer Styles**, and **Copy Layer Style**. To paste the style, select the destination layer, then click **Layer**, **Layer Styles**, and **Paste Layer Style**.

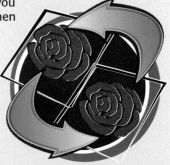

Using the Styles Palette

You can apply a custom combination of Photoshop styles to a layer to give the layer a colorful or textured look. The Styles palette offers an easy way to apply such complex effects.

① Click the **Layers** tab to select the Layers palette.

If the Layers tab is hidden, you can click **Window** and then **Layers** to open the Layers palette.

② Click the **Styles** tab to display Photoshop's styles.

If the Styles tab is hidden, you can click **Window** and then **Styles** to open the Styles palette.

③ Click a style.

● Photoshop applies the style to the selected layer.

● The style appears as a set of effects in the Layers palette.

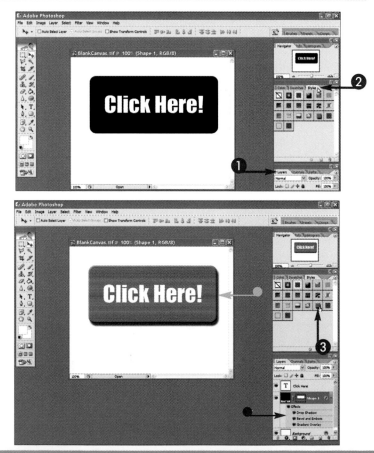

ACCESS MORE STYLES

1 Click the Styles 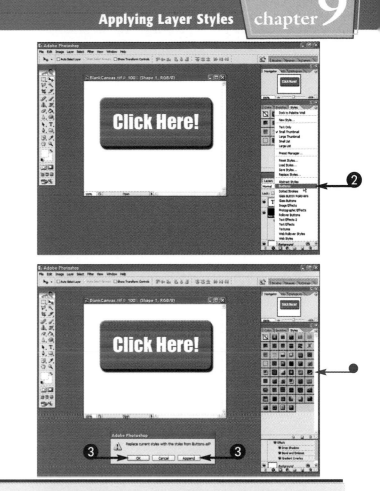.

2 Click a set of styles.

A dialog box appears and asks if you want to replace the current styles with the new set or append the new set.

3 Click **OK** or **Append**.

Photoshop places the new styles in the Styles palette.

● In this example, the new styles have been appended to the current ones.

TIP

How do I create my own custom styles?

1 Repeat steps **1** to **3** on the opposite page to apply one or more effects to a layer in your image.

Alternatively, you can apply any styles – such as Drop Shadow, Outer Glow, and others – to a layer in your image.

2 Select the layer in the Layers palette.

3 Click the Styles 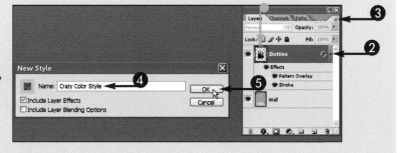 and click **New Style**.

4 In the New Style dialog box that appears, type a name for your new style.

5 Click **OK**.

● An icon for your new style appears in the Styles palette.

Applying Filters

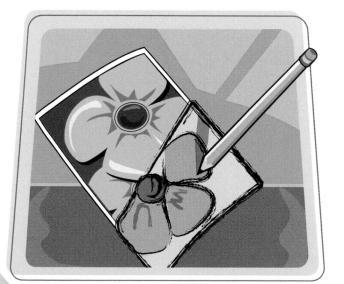

With Photoshop's filters, you can quickly and easily apply enhancements to your image, including artistic effects, texture effects, and distortions. Filters can help you correct defects in your images or enable you to turn a photograph into something resembling an impressionist painting. Photoshop comes with more than 100 filters; this chapter highlights only a few. For details about all the filters, see the Help documentation.

Turn an Image into a Painting

You can use many of Photoshop's artistic filters to make your image look as though it was created with a paintbrush. The Dry Brush filter, for example, applies a painted effect by converting similarly colored areas in your image to solid colors.

The Dry Brush filter uses the Filter Gallery interface. For more information about the Filter Gallery, see the section "Apply Multiple Filters."

Turn an Image into a Painting

① Select the layer to which you want to apply the filter.

In this example, the image has a single Background layer.

To apply the filter to just part of your image, make a selection with a selection tool.

② Click **Filter**.

③ Click **Artistic**.

④ Click **Dry Brush**.

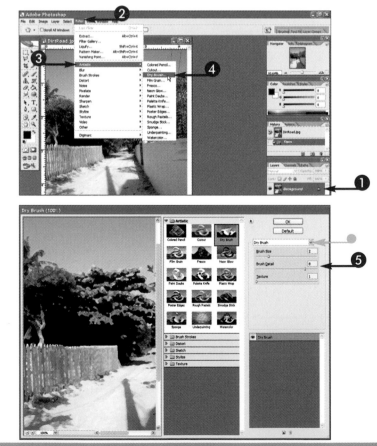

The Dry Brush dialog box appears.

The left pane displays a preview of the filter's effect.

The middle pane enables you to select a different artistic or other type of filter.

● You can also select a different filter by clicking the ⊡ in the right pane.

⑤ Fine-tune the filter effect by typing values for the **Brush Size**, **Brush Detail**, and **Texture**.

● In Windows, you can close the middle pane by clicking ⊗.

On a Mac, you can close the middle pane by clicking ▾ (▾ changes to ⊞).

This example shows how to thicken the dry-brush effect by increasing **Brush Size** and decreasing **Brush Detail**.

6 Click **OK**.

Photoshop applies the filter.

Note: For more about layers, see Chapter 8. See Chapter 4 to use the selection tools.

TIPS

What does the Sponge filter do?

The **Sponge** filter reduces detail and modifies the shapes in an image to create the effect you get when applying a damp sponge to a wet painting. Apply it by clicking **Filter**, **Artistic**, and then **Sponge**. Note that this effect is different from that of the **Sponge** tool (🔘). See Chapter 7 for more about the **Sponge** tool.

How can I make the objects in my image look like they are molded from plastic?

The **Plastic Wrap** filter gives objects a shiny appearance, as if wrapped in heat-shrink plastic. To apply this effect, click **Filter**, **Artistic**, and then **Plastic Wrap**. You can adjust how well the plastic wrap reflects light, its shininess, and its smoothness.

Photoshop's blur filters reduce the amount of detail in your image. The Gaussian Blur filter has an advantage over other blur filters in that you can control the amount of blur added.

Blur an Image

1 Select the layer to which you want to apply the filter.

In this example, the image has a single Background layer.

To apply the filter to just part of your image, make a selection with a selection tool.

2 Click **Filter**.

3 Click **Blur**.

4 Click **Gaussian Blur**.

The Gaussian Blur dialog box appears.

● A preview of the filter's effect appears here.

● You can click ⊟ or ⊞ to zoom in or out.

5 Click **Preview** to preview the effect in the main window (☐ changes to ☑).

6 Click and drag the **Radius** slider (▣) to control the amount of blur added.

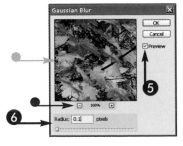

In this example, boosting the Radius value has increased the amount of blur.

7 Click **OK**.

Photoshop applies the filter.

Note: For more about layers, see Chapter 8. To use the selection tools, see Chapter 4.

How do I add directional blurring to an image?

You can add directional blur to your image with the Motion Blur filter. This can add a sense of movement to your image. To apply the filter:

1 Click **Filter**.

2 Click **Blur**.

3 Click **Motion Blur**.

4 In the Motion Blur dialog box, adjust the angle and the distance to customize the blur's direction and intensity.

5 Click **OK** to apply the filter.

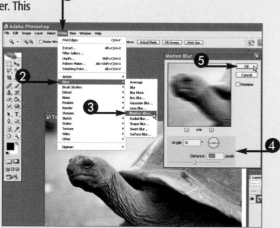

Sharpen an Image

Photoshop's sharpen filters intensify the detail and reduce blurring in your image. The Unsharp Mask filter has advantages over other sharpen filters in that you can control the amount of sharpening you apply.

1 Select the layer to which you want to apply the filter.

In this example, the filter is applied to a selection.

To apply the filter to just part of your image, make a selection with a selection tool.

2 Click **Filter**.

3 Click **Sharpen**.

4 Click **Unsharp Mask**.

The Unsharp Mask dialog box appears.

● A preview of the filter's effect appears here.

● You can click 🔲 or 🔲 to zoom out or in.

5 Click **Preview** to preview the effect in the main window (☐ changes to ☑).

6 Click and drag the sliders (🔲) to control the amount of sharpening you apply to the image.

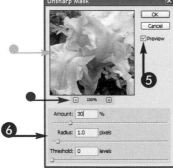

Amount controls the overall amount of sharpening.

Radius controls whether sharpening is confined to edges in the image (low Radius setting) or added across the entire image (high Radius setting).

Threshold controls how much contrast you must have present for an edge to be recognized and sharpened.

7 Click **OK**.

Photoshop applies the filter.

Note: For more about layers, see Chapter 8. To use the selection tools, see Chapter 4.

TIPS

When should I apply sharpening?

It is a good idea to sharpen an image after you have changed its size because changing an image's size can cause blurring. Applying the **Unsharp Mask** filter can also help clarify scanned images.

How can I remove a specific type of blurring from my image?

The **Smart Sharpen** filter gives you additional control over the sharpening applied to your image. You can specify that it remove blurring applied by the **Gaussian Blur**, **Lens Blur**, or **Motion Blur** filters. To access it, click **Filter**, **Sharpen**, and **Smart Sharpen**.

Photoshop's distort filters stretch and squeeze areas of your image. For example, the Spherize filter produces a fun-house effect, making your image look like it is being reflected in a mirrored sphere.

You can also distort an image by using the Distort command, located under the Image menu. See Chapter 5 for more information.

Distort an Image

① Select the layer to which you want to apply the filter.

In this example, the image has a single Background layer.

To apply the filter to just part of your image, make a selection with a selection tool.

② Click **Filter**.

③ Click **Distort**.

④ Click **Spherize**.

The Spherize dialog box appears.

● A preview of the filter's effect appears here.

● You can click ▭ or ⊞ to zoom out or in.

⑤ Click and drag the **Amount** slider (▭) to control the amount of distortion added.

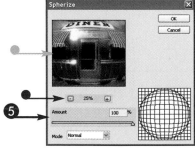

In this example, the intensity of the spherize effect has been decreased.

6 Click **OK**.

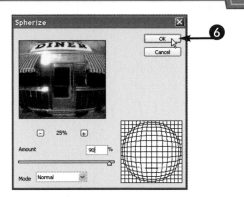

Photoshop applies the filter.

Note: *For more about layers, see Chapter 8. See Chapter 4 to use the selection tools.*

TIPS

What happens when I type a negative value in the Amount field of the Spherize dialog box?

A negative value "squeezes" the shapes in your image instead of expanding them. The **Pinch** filter — which you can also find under the **Filter** and **Distort** menu selections — produces a similar effect.

How can I quickly add wild special effects to my images?

Many of the filters in the Stylize menu produce out-of-this-world effects. The **Emboss** and **Solarize** filters are two examples. Click **Filter** and then **Stylize** to access them.

Add Noise to an Image

Filters in the Noise menu add or remove graininess in your image. You can add graininess with the Add Noise filter.

Add Noise to an Image

1 Select the layer to which you want to apply the filter.

This image has a single Background layer.

To apply the filter to just part of your image, make a selection with a selection tool.

2 Click **Filter**.

3 Click **Noise**.

4 Click **Add Noise**.

The Add Noise dialog box opens.

● A preview appears here.

● You can click ▣ or ⊞ to zoom out or in.

5 Click **Preview** to preview the effect in the main window (☐ changes to ☑).

6 Click and drag the ▢ to control the amount of noise added.

7 Select the way you want the noise distributed (○ changes to ◉).

The **Uniform** option spreads the noise more evenly than the **Gaussian** option.

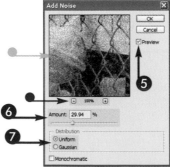

In this example, the **Amount** value has been increased.

8 Click **OK**.

Photoshop applies the filter.

Note: *For more about layers, see Chapter 8. See Chapter 4 to use the selection tools.*

TIP

What does the Monochromatic setting in the Add Noise dialog box do?

If you click **Monochromatic** (☐ changes to ☑), Photoshop adds noise by lightening or darkening pixels in your image. Pixel hues stay the same. At high settings with the Monochromatic setting on, the filter produces a television-static effect.

Turn an Image into Shapes

The pixelate filters divide areas of your image into solid-colored dots or shapes. The Crystallize filter, one example of a pixelate filter, re-creates your image using colored polygons.

Turn an Image into Shapes

① Select the layer to which you want to apply the filter.

In this example, the image has a single Background layer.

To apply the filter to just part of your image, make a selection with a selection tool.

② Click **Filter**.

③ Click **Pixelate**.

④ Click **Crystallize**.

The Crystallize dialog box appears.

● A preview of the filter's effect appears here.

● You can click ☐ or ☐ to zoom out or in.

⑤ Click and drag the **Cell Size** slider (☐) to adjust the size of the shapes.

The size can range from 3 to 300.

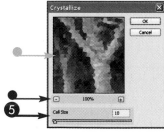

In this example, the **Cell Size** has been slightly increased.

6 Click **OK**.

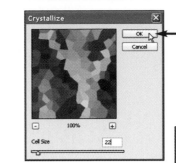

Photoshop applies the filter.

Note: *For more about layers, see Chapter 8. To use the selection tools, see Chapter 4.*

What does the Mosaic filter do?

The **Mosaic** filter converts your image to a set of solid-color squares. You can control the size of the squares in the filter's dialog box. Apply the filter by clicking **Filter**, **Pixelate**, and then **Mosaic**.

What does the Stained Glass filter do?

The **Stained Glass** filter converts small areas of your image to different solid-color shapes, similar to those you may see in a stained-glass window. A foreground-color border separates the shapes. You can adjust the thickness of the border, along with cell size and light intensity. Apply this filter by selecting **Filter**, **Texture**, and then **Stained Glass**.

Turn an Image into a Charcoal Sketch

The sketch filters add outlining effects to your image. The Charcoal filter, for example, makes an image look as if you have sketched it by using charcoal on paper.

Photoshop uses the foreground and background colors from the Toolbox as the charcoal and paper colors, respectively. Changing these colors changes the filter's effect. See Chapter 7 to adjust color.

The Charcoal filter uses the Filter Gallery interface. For more information about the Filter Gallery, see the section "Apply Multiple Filters."

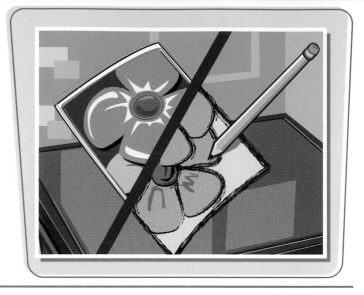

Turn an Image into a Charcoal Sketch

① Select the layer to which you want to apply the filter.

In this example, the image has a single Background layer.

To apply the filter to just part of your image, make a selection with a selection tool.

② Click **Filter**.

③ Click **Sketch**.

④ Click **Charcoal**.

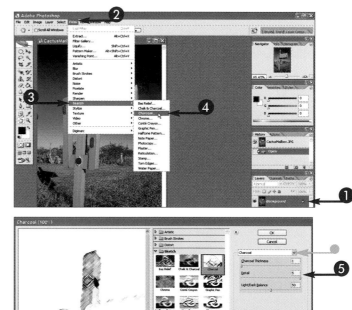

The Charcoal dialog box appears.

The left pane displays a preview of the filter's effect.

The middle pane enables you to select a different sketch or other type of filter.

● You can also select a different filter by clicking the ⊠ in the right pane.

⑤ Click and drag the sliders (⬜) to control the filter's effect.

● In Windows, you can close the middle pane by clicking ⊗.

On a Mac, you can close the middle pane by clicking ▾ (▾ changes to ◧).

In this example, the thickness of the charcoal strokes has been increased. The **Light/Dark Balance** setting has also been increased.

6 Click **OK**.

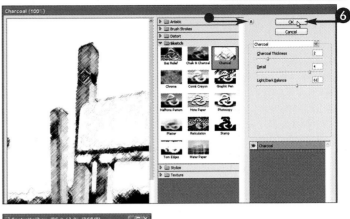

Photoshop applies the filter.

Note: *For more about layers, see Chapter 8. To use the selection tools, see Chapter 4.*

What does the Photocopy filter do?

The Photocopy filter converts shadows and midtones in your image to the foreground color in the Toolbox and highlights in your image to the background color. The result is an image that looks photocopied. To apply the Photocopy filter:

1 Follow steps **1** to **4** in this section, but in step **4**, select **Photocopy**.

The Filter Gallery appears with the Photocopy filter selected.

2 Adjust the detail and the darkness of the filter effect.

3 Click **OK**.

Photoshop applies the filter.

Apply Glowing Edges to an Image

The Glowing Edges filter, one example of a stylize filter, applies a neon effect to the edges in your image. Areas between the edges turn black. Other stylize filters produce similarly extreme artistic effects.

The Glowing Edges filter uses the Filter Gallery interface. For more information about the Filter Gallery, see the section "Apply Multiple Filters."

Apply Glowing Edges to an Image

① Select the layer to which you want to apply the filter.

In this example, the image has a single Background layer.

To apply the filter to just part of your image, make a selection with a selection tool.

② Click **Filter**.

③ Click **Stylize**.

④ Click **Glowing Edges**.

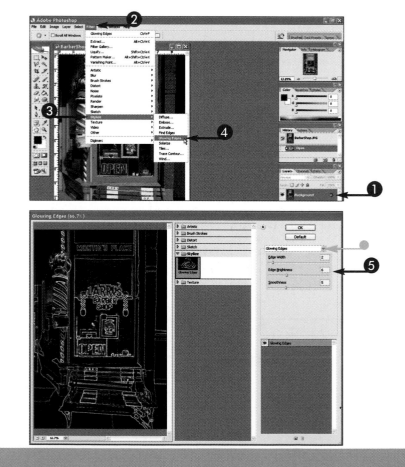

The Glowing Edges dialog box appears.

The left pane displays a preview of the filter's effect.

The middle pane enables you to select a different filter.

● You can also select a different filter by clicking the ⊠ in the right pane.

⑤ Click and drag the sliders (⬜) to control the intensity of the glow you add to the edges in the image.

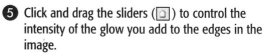

● In Windows, you can close the middle pane by clicking 🔼.

On a Mac, you can close the middle pane by clicking ▼ (▼ changes to ⬛).

In this example, the **Edge Width** and **Edge Brightness** values have been increased to intensify the neon effect.

6 Click **OK**.

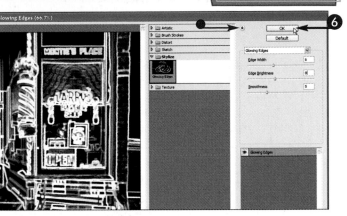

Photoshop applies the filter.

Note: *For more about layers, see Chapter 8. To use the selection tools, see Chapter 4.*

What is the Find Edges filter?

The Find Edges filter is similar to the Glowing Edges filter except that it places white pixels between the edges in your image. Find Edges is a one-step filter, which means that you cannot fine-tune its effects in a dialog box before you apply it. To apply the filter:

1 Click **Filter**.

2 Click **Stylize**.

3 Click **Find Edges**.

Photoshop applies the filter.

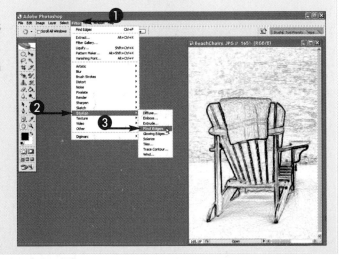

You can overlay different textures on your image with the Texturizer filter. The other texture filters enable you to apply other patterns.

The Dry Brush filter uses the Filter Gallery interface. For more information about the Filter Gallery, see "Apply Multiple Filters."

1 Select the layer to which you want to apply the filter.

In this example, the filter is applied to a selection.

To apply the filter to just part of your image, make a selection with a selection tool.

2 Click **Filter**.

3 Click **Texture**.

4 Click **Texturizer**.

The Texturizer dialog box appears.

The left pane displays a preview of the filter's effect.

The middle pane enables you to select a different texture or other type of filter.

● You can also select a different filter by clicking the ⊻ in the right pane.

5 Click here and select a texture to apply.

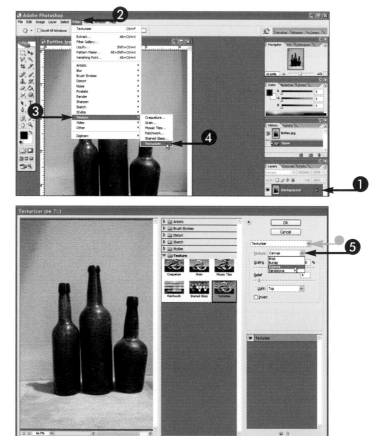

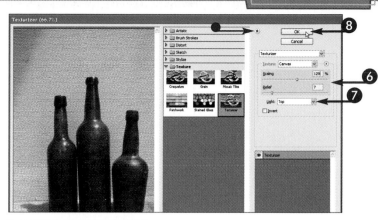

6 Click and drag the sliders () to control the size and intensity of the overlaid texture.

7 Click here and select a **Light** direction.

● In Windows, you can close the middle pane by clicking 🔼.

On a Mac, you can close the middle pane by clicking 🔽 (🔽 changes to 🔼).

8 Click **OK**.

Photoshop applies the filter.

Note: For more about layers, see Chapter 8. See Chapter 4 to use the selection tools.

TIP

What is a lens flare, and how can I add it to an image?

Lens flare is the extra flash of light that appears in a photo when too much light enters a camera lens. Photographers try to avoid this effect, but you can add it to make your image look like an old-fashioned photograph. To apply the filter:

1 Click **Filter**.

2 Click **Render**.

3 Click **Lens Flare**.

4 In the Lens Flare dialog box, click and drag 🔲 to control the brightness.

5 Click and drag ✛ to position the lens flare in your image.

6 Click **OK** to apply the filter.

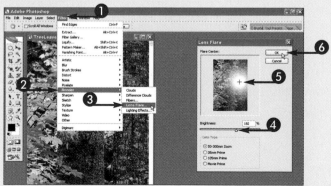

Offset an Image

The filters in the Other submenu produce interesting effects that do not fall under the other menu descriptions. For example, you can shift your image horizontally or vertically in the image window using the Other submenu's Offset filter.

Offset an Image

1. Select the layer to which you want to apply the filter.

   In this example, the image has a single Background layer.

   To apply the filter to just part of your image, make a selection with a selection tool.

2. Click **Filter**.

3. Click **Other**.

4. Click **Offset**.

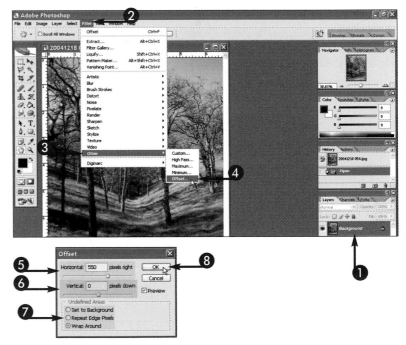

   The Offset dialog box appears.

5. Type a horizontal offset.

6. Type a vertical offset.

7. Select how you want Photoshop to treat pixels at the edge (○ changes to ◉).

8. Click **OK**.

In this example, the image has been shifted horizontally to the right by typing a positive value in the horizontal field.

Wrap Around was selected in step **7**, so the pixels cropped from the right edge of the image reappear on the left edge.

In this example, the same offset was applied but with **Repeat Edge Pixels** selected in step **7**. This creates a streaked effect at the left edge.

Note: For more about layers, see Chapter 8. See Chapter 4 to use the selection tools.

TIP

How do I make a seamless tile?

Seamless tiles are images that when laid side by side leave no noticeable seam where they meet. They are often used as background images for Web pages. To create a seamless tile, start with an evenly textured image, offset the image horizontally and vertically, and clean up the resulting seams with the **Clone Stamp** tool (⟦⟧). See Chapter 6 for information on using the **Clone Stamp** tool. The resulting image tiles seamlessly when you use it as a Web page background.

Photoshop's Liquify tools enable you to dramatically warp areas of your image. The tools are useful for making your image look like it is melting.

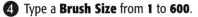

① Select the layer to which you want to apply the Liquify filter.

In this example, the image has a single Background layer.

To apply the filter to just part of your image, make a selection with a selection tool.

② Click **Filter**.

③ Click **Liquify**.

The Liquify dialog box appears.

④ Type a **Brush Size** from **1** to **600**.

⑤ Type a **Brush Pressure**, or strength, from **1** to **100**.

⑥ Click a liquify tool.

This example uses the **Forward Warp** tool (⬚).

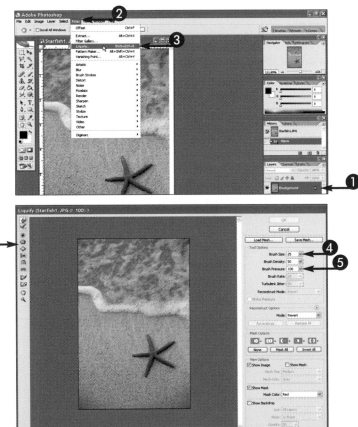

⑦ Click and drag inside the image preview box.

Photoshop liquifies the image where you drag the brush.

● You can click **Reconstruct** to change the image back to its original state, step by step.

● You can click the **Show Mesh** option (☐ changes to ☑) to overlay a grid to measure your changes.

⑧ Click **OK**.

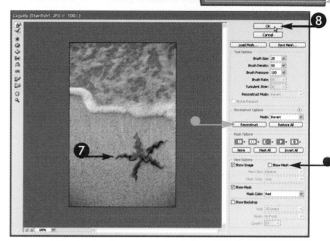

Photoshop applies the Liquify effect to your image.

Note: For more about layers, see Chapter 8. See Chapter 4 to use the selection tools.

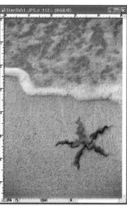

TIP

What do some of the different liquify tools do?

	Forward Warp tool	Pushes pixels in the direction you drag.
	Reconstruct tool	Restores pixels to their original state.
	Twirl Clockwise tool	Twirls pixels clockwise. You can press Alt (Option) as you apply the tool to twirl pixels counterclockwise.
	Pucker tool	Pushes pixels toward the brush center.
	Bloat tool	Pushes pixels away from the brush center.
	Push Left tool	Pushes pixels to the left of the cursor as you drag.
	Mirror tool	Reflects pixels as you drag.
	Turbulence tool	Mimics a roiling liquid.

Apply Multiple Filters

You can apply more than one filter to an image using the Filter Gallery interface. The interface enables you to view a variety of filter effects and apply them in combination.

Many filters bring up the Filter Gallery interface when you apply them, including Dry Brush, Charcoal Sketch, Glowing Edges, and Texturizer. See previous sections in this chapter for more information about these filters.

Not all of the effects listed under Photoshop's Filter menu appear in the Filter Gallery.

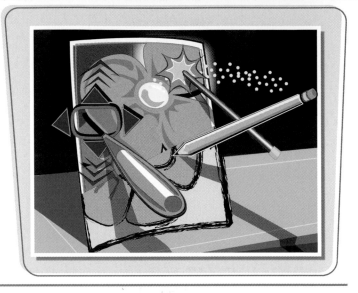

Apply Multiple Filters

① Select the layer to which you want to apply the filters.

In this example, the image has a single Background layer.

To apply the filters to just part of your image, make a selection with a selection tool.

② Click **Filter**.

③ Click **Filter Gallery**.

The Filter Gallery dialog box appears with the most recently applied filter selected.

The left pane displays a preview of the filtered image.

④ Click 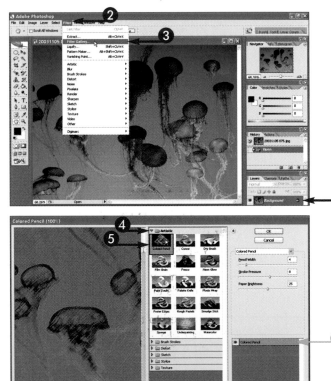 to display filters from a category (□ changes to ▣).

⑤ Click a thumbnail to apply a filter.

● The filter appears in the filter list.

⑥ Click the **New Effect Layer** button (▣).

⑦ Click 🗁 to display filters from another category.

⑧ Click a thumbnail to apply another filter.

You can repeat steps **6** to **8** to apply additional filters.

⑨ Click **OK**.

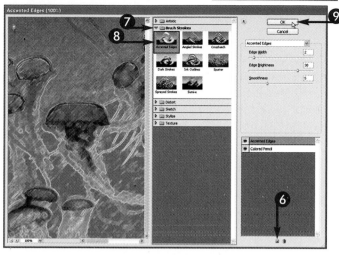

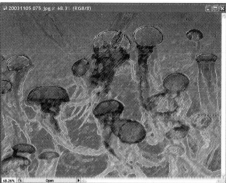

Photoshop applies the filters.

Note: *For more about layers, see Chapter 8. See Chapter 4 to use the selection tools.*

TIP

How can I turn off filters in the Filter Gallery?

Currently applied filters appear in a list in the lower-right corner of the Filter Gallery. You can click 👁 to temporarily hide a filter in the list. A hidden filter's effects are not applied to the preview in the left pane of the Filter Gallery, nor are they applied to the image when you click **OK**. You can click the 🗑 icon to delete a filter entirely from the list.

Generate a Pattern

You can generate an abstract pattern based on a selection in your image using Photoshop's Pattern Maker. The Pattern Maker enables you to specify the size, border color, and other settings for your pattern.

You can use your patterns as backgrounds on Web pages.

① Open the image from which you want to generate the pattern.

② Click **Filter**.

③ Click **Pattern Maker**.

The Pattern Maker dialog box appears.

④ Click the **Rectangular Marquee** tool (▭).

⑤ Click and drag inside the image to select an area from which to generate your pattern.

⑥ Type the dimensions for your pattern.

If the dimensions are smaller than the image dimensions, the pattern repeats.

7 Click here and specify the smoothness of the pattern.

8 Click here and specify the size of the details in the pattern.

● You can click **Tile Boundaries** to add a border around the pattern (☐ changes to ☑).

● You can click the color box to select the color of the border.

9 Click **Generate**.

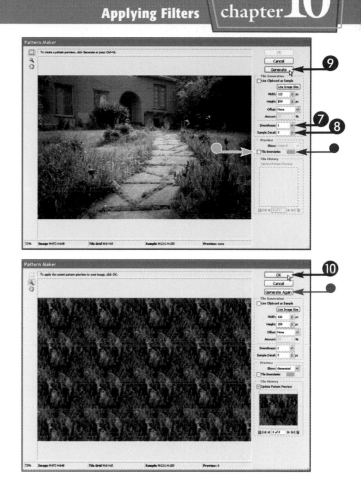

Photoshop generates the pattern.

● You can click **Generate Again** to create a new pattern.

10 Click **OK**.

The pattern appears in the image window.

TIP

How can I view patterns that Photoshop has already generated?

When you click **Generate** to create new patterns in the Pattern Maker, Photoshop remembers previous patterns, up to a total of 20. To cycle through previous patterns, you can click the following buttons, located in the Tile History area of the dialog box:

⏮	Click to view the first pattern.
◀	Click to view the previous pattern.
▶	Click to view the next pattern.
⏭	Click to view the last pattern.

CHAPTER 11

Drawing Shapes

Photoshop offers a variety of tools for drawing geometric and abstract shapes. Other tools let you edit the lines that bound your shapes, or change the colors with which the shapes are filled. You can also use the tools to draw lines that have arrowheads at their ends.

You can create solid shapes in
your image using Photoshop's
many shape tools. These tools
make it easy to create geometric
decorations for your photos or
buttons for your Web site.

Draw a Shape

DRAW A SOLID SHAPE

1 Click the **Shape** tool (⬭).

Note: The tool icon may differ, depending on the shape you drew last.

2 Click a shape in the Options bar.

3 Make sure you select the **Shape Layers** icon (▣)
in the Options bar.

4 Click the **Color** box to select a fill color for the
shape.

Note: For details on selecting colors, see Chapter 6.

5 Click and drag to draw the shape.

Photoshop draws the shape and fills it with the
specified color.

● The shape appears in a new layer in the Layers
palette.

Note: For more about layers, see Chapter 8.

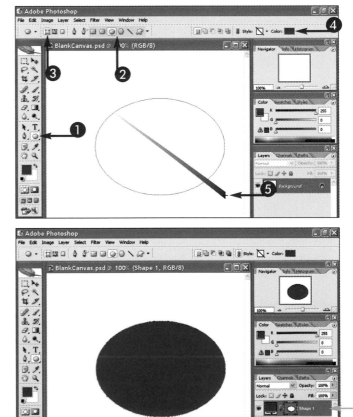

DRAW A STYLIZED SHAPE

① Click a shape button.

② Click here and then select a style for your shape.

Photoshop offers a variety of colorful 3-D styles.

③ Click and drag to draw the shape.

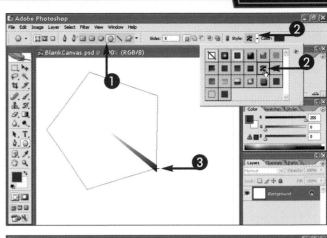

Photoshop draws the shape and applies the specified style.

● The shape appears in a new layer in the Layers palette.

Note: For more about layers, see Chapter 8. For more about styles, see Chapter 9.

● You can move the shape by selecting its layer and using the **Move** tool (⊕).

Note: For more about the Move tool, see Chapter 5.

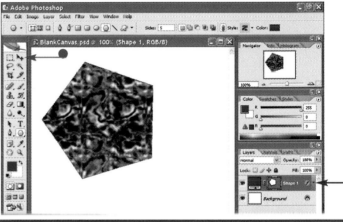

 TIPS

How do I resize a shape after I draw it?

Click the shape's layer and then click the **Shape** tool (🔲). Click **Edit**, click **Transform Path**, and then click a transform command. You can then resize the shape just as you would a selection. See Chapter 5 for details on transforming selections.

How do I overlap shapes in interesting ways?

To determine how overlapping shapes interact, click one of the following options in the Options bar before drawing:

Tool Name	Description
Add to Shape Area (🔲)	Combines a shape area with another shape area
Subtract from Shape Area (🔲)	Cuts a shape area out of another shape area
Intersect Shape Areas (🔲)	Keeps the area where shapes intersect
Exclude Overlapping Shape Areas (🔲)	Keeps the area where shapes do not overlap

Draw a Custom Shape

You can use the Custom Shape tool to draw a variety of interesting predefined shapes, including animals, frames, and talk bubbles.

Draw a Custom Shape

1. Click 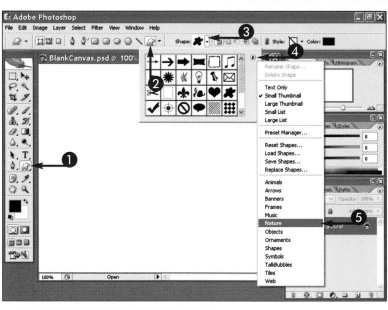.

2. Click the **Custom Shape** button (🖾) in the Options bar.

3. Click the **Shape** ⬇.

4. Click the **Option** arrow (⊙).

5. Click a shape category.

A dialog box appears and asks if you want to replace the current shapes.

- You can click **Append** to append the new shapes to the current shapes.

6. Click **OK**.

Photoshop replaces the old shapes with your current shapes.

7 Click a shape.

8 Click the **Color** box to select a color for the shape.

Note: For details on selecting colors, see Chapter 6.

9 Click and drag to draw the shape.

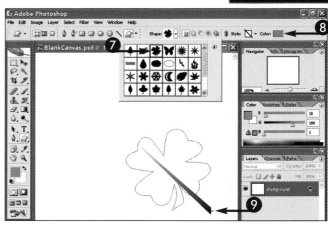

Photoshop draws the shape and fills it with the specified color.

● The shape appears in a new layer in the Layers palette.

Note: For more about layers, see Chapter 8.

● You can move the shape by selecting its layer and using .

Note: For more about the Move tool, see Chapter 5.

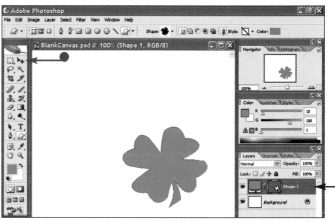

TIPS

How do I apply a shadow behind a shape?

You can apply a Drop Shadow style to the shape. Select your shape layer in the Layers palette, and then click **Layer**, **Layer Style**, and **Drop Shadow**. A dialog box appears that enables you to customize the shadowing. For more about applying styles, see Chapter 9.

How do I overlay text on a shape?

You can select the **Type** tool (**T**), click on your shape, and then type the text you want to overlay. This can be useful when you want to label buttons that you have created with the Shape tool. You will probably want to select a color for your text that contrasts with the color of your shape. For more about applying type, see Chapter 12.

Draw a Straight Line

You can draw a straight line using Photoshop's Shape tool. You can customize the line with arrowheads, giving you an easy way to point out elements in your image.

① Click 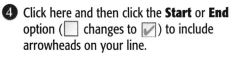.

Note: *The tool icon may differ, depending on the shape you drew last.*

② Make sure you select ▣ in the Options bar.

③ Click the **Line** icon (◰).

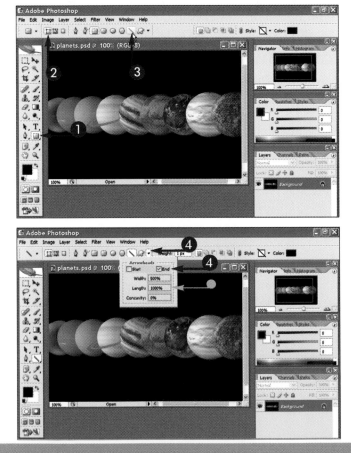

④ Click here and then click the **Start** or **End** option (☐ changes to ☑) to include arrowheads on your line.

● You can also specify the size and shape of the arrowheads by typing values here.

⑤ Press Enter (Return on a Mac) to close the menu.

6 Type a line weight.

7 Click here and then click a style for your line.

● The **Default** style (⬛) creates a plain, solid line.

8 Press **Enter** (**Return** on a Mac) to close the menu.

● You can click the **Color** box to select a different line color.

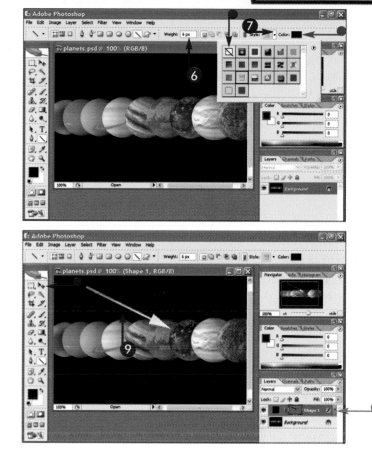

9 Click and drag to draw the line.

● Photoshop places the line in its own layer.

Note: For more about layers, see Chapter 8.

● You can move the shape by selecting its layer and using ⬛.

Note: For more about the Move tool, see Chapter 5.

How do I draw a horizontal or vertical line?
Press **Shift** as you click and drag to create your line. You can also use this technique to drag lines at 45-degree angles.

How do I resize a line?
You can select the layer containing the line, click **Image**, and then click **Free Transform**. A bounding box appears around the line. You can click and drag the handles on the sides and corners to resize the line.

Draw a Shape with the Pen

With the Pen tool, you can create shapes by drawing the lines yourself. This enables you to make shapes that are not included in Photoshop's predefined menus.

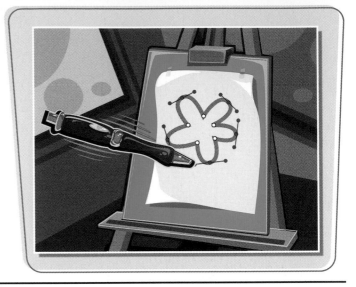

USING THE REGULAR PEN

1 Click the **Pen** tool (![pen icon]).

2 Click the **Color** box to select a color for the shape.

Note: For details on selecting colors, see Chapter 6.

3 Click inside your image to set an initial anchor point.

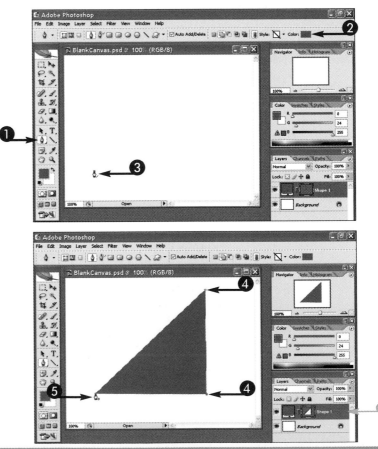

4 Continue clicking to set additional anchor points to define the shape.

5 Click the initial anchor point to close the shape.

Photoshop draws a straight-sided shape.

● Photoshop places the shape in its own layer.

You can ceate curred paths if you click and draw with ![pen icon].

USING THE FREEFORM PEN

① Click and hold .

② Click **Freeform Pen Tool** (✎) from the list that appears.

● You can also select the tool from the Options bar.

③ Click and drag inside your image.

Photoshop draws a free-form line.

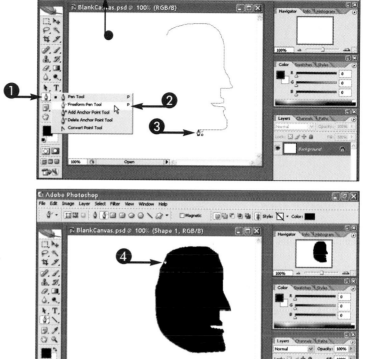

④ Drag to the starting point of the line.

Photoshop completes the shape.

Alternatively, you can release the mouse, and Photoshop completes your shape with a straight line.

● Photoshop places the shape in its own layer.

TIP

Can I use the Pen tool to trace an object?
If the object has well-defined edges, you can trace it using the **Freeform Pen** tool with the **Magnetic** option selected in the Options bar (☐ changes to ✓). The tool works similarly to the **Magnetic Lasso** tool (✎). For more on using the Magnetic Lasso tool, see Chapter 4.

Edit a Shape

You can edit shapes by manipulating their anchor points. This lets you fine-tune the geometries of your shapes.

You can edit shapes drawn with Photoshop's predefined shape tools or the Pen tool.

For more shape-editing techniques, see Photoshop's Help documentation.

MOVE AN ANCHOR POINT

① Click and hold the **Path Selection** tool (⬚).

② Click **Direct Selection Tool** (⬚) from the list that appears.

③ Click the edge of a shape to select it.

Photoshop shows the anchor points that make up the shape.

④ Click and drag an anchor point.

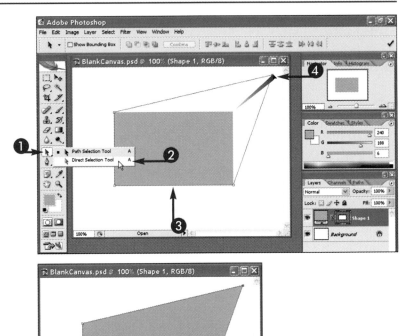

Photoshop moves the anchor point, changing the geometry of the shape.

BEND A STRAIGHT SEGMENT

① Click and hold .

② Click **Add Anchor Point Tool** () from the list that appears.

③ Click a straight line between two anchor points.

Photoshop adds an anchor point to the line.

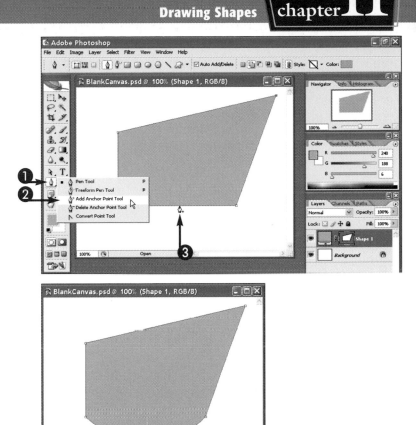

④ Click the anchor point and drag.

⑤ Release the mouse.

Photoshop turns the straight line into a curved line.

You can use this technique to create a concave or convex curve.

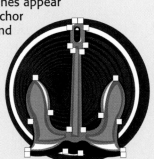

How do I edit curved lines?

If you click an anchor point situated on a curved line with the **Direct Selection** tool (), direction lines appear to the sides of the anchor point. You can click and drag the ends of the direction lines to edit the curve on each side of the anchor point. You can also click and drag the curves themselves with the .

How do I turn a shape layer into a regular layer?

You can turn a shape layer into a regular layer by *rasterizing* it. Click the shape layer, then click **Layer**, **Rasterize**, and then **Shape**. After rasterizing, the shape's anchor points are no longer accessible. This means you cannot change the dimensions of the shape by editing the anchor points. Most of Photoshop's filter commands require you to rasterize a shape before you can apply the commands to it. For more about filters, see Chapter 10.

CHAPTER

12

Adding and Manipulating Type

Add Tex

Do you want to add letters and words to your photos and illustrations? Photoshop lets you add type to your images and precisely control the type's appearance and layout. You can also modify your type using Photoshop's styles.

Add Type to an Image

Adding type enables you to label elements in your image or use letters and words in artistic ways.

① Click the **Type** tool (☐).

② Click where you want the new type to appear.

Note: You can also create a bounding box by drawing a shape. See Chapter 11 for details.

③ Click ☑ and select a font, style, and size for your type.

④ Click the color swatch to select a color for your type.

Note: Photoshop applies the foreground color by default. See Chapter 6 for more about selecting colors.

5 Type your text.

To create a line break, press **Enter** (**Return** on a Mac).

6 When you finish typing your text, click ☑ or press **Enter** on your keyboard's number pad.

● Photoshop places the type in its own layer.

● You can click the alignment buttons to left-align (▤), center (▤), or right-align (▤) your type.

 TIPS

How do I create vertical type?

If you click and hold the **Type** tool (T), a list that contains the **Vertical Type** tool (IT) appears. You can then use the tool to create up-and-down type. When using the regular **Type** tool, you can click the **Change Orientation** button (IT) in the Options bar to change horizontal type to vertical, and vice versa. Note that with vertical type, "lines" go from right to left.

How do I reposition my type?

You can use the **Move** tool (▶⊕) to move the layer that contains the type. Click that layer, click ▶⊕, and then click and drag to reposition your type. For more about moving a layer, see Chapter 8.

Add Type in a Bounding Box

You can add type inside a *bounding box* to constrain where the type appears and how it wraps.

① Click **T**.

② Click and drag inside the image to define the bounding box.

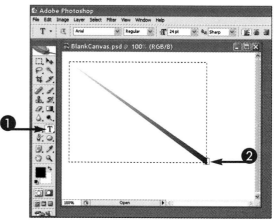

③ Click and drag the handles (☐) of the bounding box to adjust its dimensions.

④ Click and drag the center point (⊕) of the bounding box to move the box.

⑤ Click ▾ and select the formatting of the type to be added.

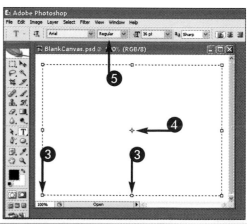

6 Type your text.

Your text appears inside the bounding box.

When a line of text hits the edge of the bounding box, it automatically wraps to the next line. Photoshop also automatically adds hyphenation.

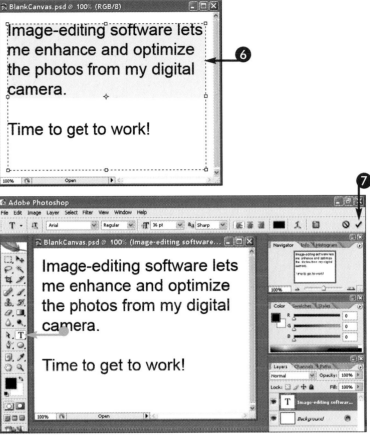

7 When you finish typing your text, click ✔ or press **Enter** on your keyboard's number pad.

The bounding box disappears.

● To make the box reappear in order to change its dimensions, click T and click the text.

TIP

How do I format paragraph text inside a bounding box?

Follow these steps:

1 Click T.

2 Click the text inside the box.

3 Click **Window**.

4 Click **Paragraph**.

The Paragraph palette appears.

5 Type values or click the various tools to control the alignment, indenting, and hyphenation of the text inside a bounding box.

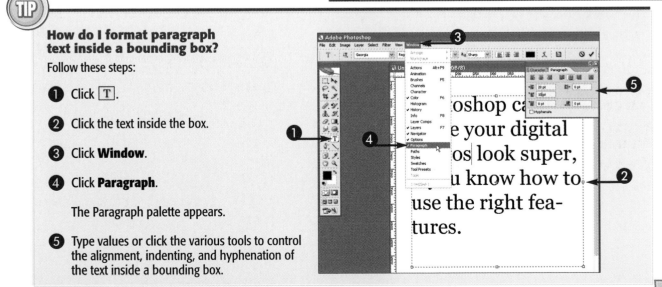

Change the Formatting of Type

You can change the font, style, size, and other characteristics of your type.

1. Click T.
2. Click the type layer that you want to edit.

   If the Layers palette is not visible, you can click **Window** and then **Layers** to view it.
3. Click and drag to select some type.
4. Click the font menu.

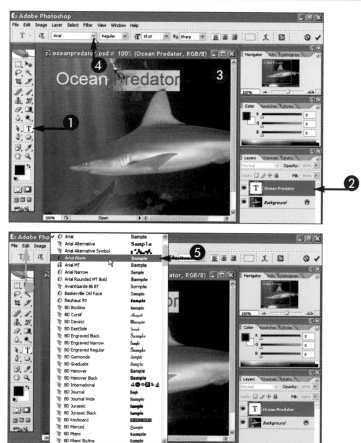

Photoshop displays the names of fonts that are available along with previews.

● You can change the size of the font previews in the Type preferences dialog box by clicking **Edit**, **Preferences**, and then **Type**.

5. Click a font.

6 Click here and select the type's style.

7 Click here and select the type's size.

● You can edit your type in more complex ways by clicking **Window** and then **Character** to open the Character palette.

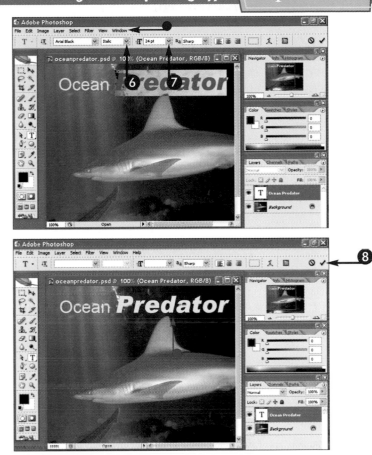

8 When you finish formatting your text, click ✓ or press Enter on your keyboard's number pad.

● Photoshop applies the formatting to your type.

TIPS

How do I edit the content of my type?

With the type's layer selected in the Layers palette, you can click inside the text with the **Type** tool (T). Then you can press Delete to delete letters, and type to add new ones. You can press ←, →, ↑, or ↓ to move the cursor inside your type.

How can I check the spelling of my text?

Select your type layer in the Layers palette, click **Edit**, and then click **Check Spelling**. Photoshop compares your text with the text in its dictionary. It flags words it does not recognize and suggests replacements.

Change the Color of Type

You can change the color of your type to make it blend or contrast with the rest of the image.

① Click T.

② Click the type layer that you want to edit.

If the Layers palette is not visible, you can click **Window** and then **Layers** to view it.

③ Click and drag to select some text.

● You can double-click the layer thumbnail to select all the type.

④ Click the Color swatch in the Options bar.

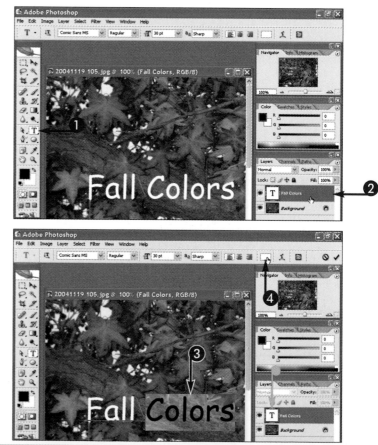

The Color Picker dialog box appears.

⑤ Click a color.

● You can click and drag the slider () to change the colors that Photoshop displays in the selection box.

⑥ Click **OK**.

⑦ Click ✔ or press **Enter** on your keyboard's number pad.

● Photoshop changes the text to the new color.

TIPS

What is anti-aliasing?

Anti-aliasing is the process of adding semitransparent pixels to curved edges in digital images to make the edges appear smoother. You can apply anti-aliasing to type to improve its appearance. Text that you do not anti-alias can sometimes look jagged. You can control the presence and style of your type's anti-aliasing with the ▣ menu in the Options bar.

How can I apply a color gradient to my type?

You can apply a Gradient Overlay style to your type layer. Click the type layer, then click **Layer**, **Layer Style**, and **Gradient Overlay**. A dialog box appears allowing you to define the gradient settings. For more about styles, see Chapter 9.

Apply a Style to Type

You can easily apply a style to type to give it a colorful or 3-D appearance. After you apply a style, you can still edit the type using the type tools.

For more about styles, see Chapter 9.

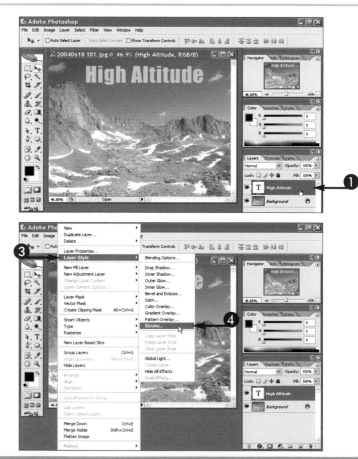

① Select the type layer to which you want to apply a style.

   If the Layers palette is not visible, you can click **Window** and then **Layers** to view it.

② Click **Layer**.

③ Click **Layer Style**.

④ Click a style.

   You can also click the **f circle** icon (⬤) in the Layers palette to select a style.

The Layer Style dialog box appears.

5 Adjust the settings to produce the effect you want.

● You can apply multiple styles by clicking the options (□ changes to ☑) on the left.

Note: See Chapter 9 for details.

6 Click **OK**.

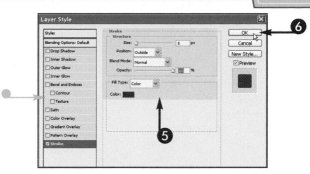

● Photoshop applies the style to the type.

● You can click here to display the styles.

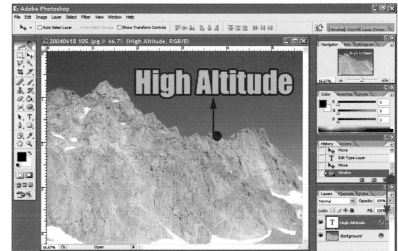

TIPS

How do I convert my type to a shape?

Click the type layer in the Layers palette. Then click **Layer**, **Type**, and **Convert to Shape**. After you convert your type to a shape, you can edit the outline of the type using the **Direct Selection** tool (▶) and other shape tools. For more about editing shapes, see Chapter 11.

How can I create semitransparent type?

Select the type layer in the Layers palette and then reduce the layer's opacity to less than 100%. This makes the type semitransparent. For details about changing opacity, see Chapter 8.

Warp Type

You can easily bend and distort layers of type with Photoshop's Warp feature. This can make words look wrinkled, or like they are blowing in the wind.

Warp Type

① Click ⊤.

② Click the type layer that you want to warp.

   If the Layers palette is not visible, you can click **Window** and then **Layers** to view it.

③ Click the **Create Warped Text** button (⊿).

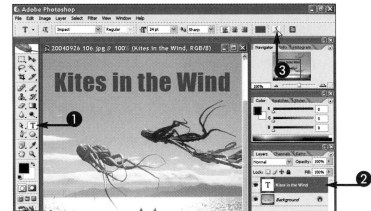

The Warp Text dialog box appears.

④ Click the **Style** ✓ (☷ on a Mac).

⑤ Click a warp style.

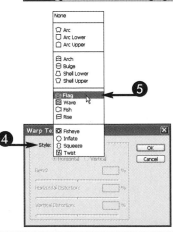

⑥ Click an orientation for the warp effect
(○ changes to ◉).

⑦ Adjust the Bend and Distortion values by
clicking and dragging the sliders (▢).

The Bend and Distortion values determine
the strength of the warp. At 0% for all
values, no warp is applied.

⑧ Click **OK**.

● Photoshop warps the text.

You can still edit the format, color, and other
characteristics of the type after you apply
the warp.

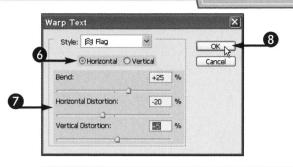

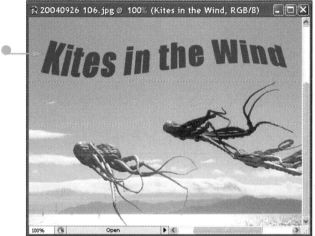

TIP

How do I unwarp text?
Follow these steps:

❶ Click the type layer that
you want to unwarp.

❷ Click the **Warp Text** button (▨).

❸ In the Warp Text dialog box, click
the Style ▾ (▦) and select **None**.

❹ Click **OK**.

Photoshop unwarps your type.

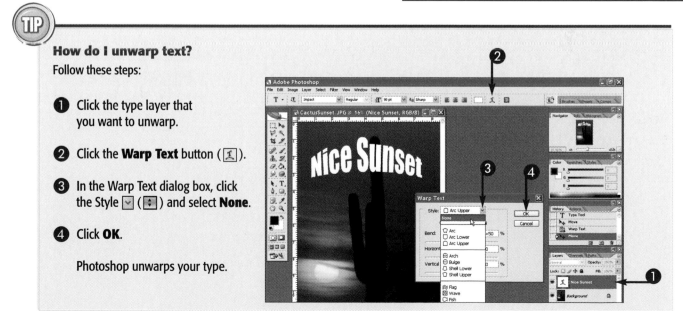

CHAPTER 13

Automating Your Work

Sometimes you want to perform the same simple sequence of commands on many different images. With Photoshop's action commands, you can automate repetitive imaging tasks by saving sequences of commands and applying them automatically to many image files. Other Photoshop commands enable you to streamline your work by helping you create Web photo galleries, picture packages, contact sheets, and panoramas.

You can record a sequence of commands as an action and replay it on other image files. This can save you time when you have a task in Photoshop that you need to repeat.

Once you record an action, you can play it. See the section "Play an Action" for more information.

Record an Action

① Click **Window**.

② Click **Actions**.

The Actions palette opens.

③ Click the **Create New Action** button ([⬚]) to open the New Action dialog box.

④ Type a name for your action.

⑤ Click **Record**.

⑥ Perform the sequence of commands that you want to automate on your images.

● In this example, the first command, Auto Contrast, is performed by clicking **Image**, **Adjustments**, and then **Auto Contrast**.

Note: See Chapter 7 for more about adjusting colors and contrast.

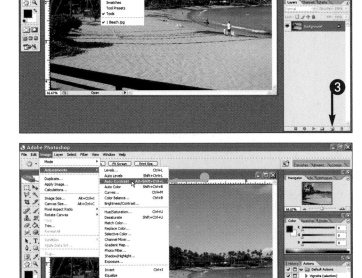

● In this example, the second command is performed by clicking **Image** and **Image Size**, then reducing the image size to 80%.

Note: See Chapter 3 for more about resizing images.

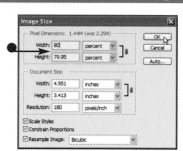

7 Click the **Stop** button (■) to stop recording.

● The Actions palette lists the commands performed under the name of the action.

TIPS

What if I make a mistake when recording my action?

You can try recording the action again by clicking the **Options** arrow (▣) in the Actions palette and clicking **Record Again**. This runs through the same actions, and you can apply different settings in the command dialog boxes. Alternatively, you can select the action, click the **Trash** icon (🗑) to delete the action, and try rerecording it.

How can I control how fast the steps of an action are performed?

In the Actions palette, click the **Options** arrow (▣) and then **Playback Options**. A dialog box appears enabling you to insert a pause after each step of an action. This can help you to understand how a complicated action is performed. The default behavior in Photoshop is to complete the actions as fast as possible.

Play an Action

You can play an action from the Actions palette on an image. This saves time, because you can execute multiple Photoshop commands with a single click. You can also play a specific command that is part of an action by itself.

Play an Action

① Click **Window**.

② Click **Actions**.

The Actions palette opens.

Photoshop comes with several predefined actions in the Actions palette.

Note: To create your own action, see the section "Record an Action."

③ Click the action that you want to play.

④ Click the **Play** button (▶).

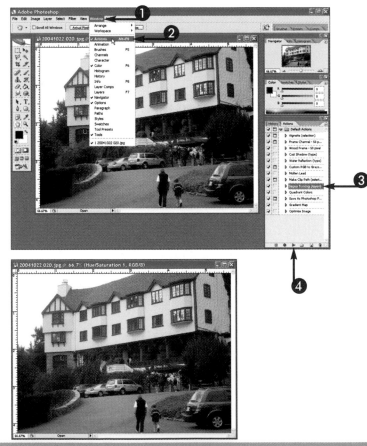

Photoshop applies the action's commands to the image.

In this example, a sepia tone is applied to the image.

You can undo the multiple commands in an action using the History palette.

Note: See Chapter 2 for more information.

PLAY A COMMAND IN AN ACTION

1 In the Actions palette, click ▷ to list the commands that make up an action (▷ changes to ▽).

2 Click the command that you want to execute.

You can press **Shift** +click to select multiple commands.

3 Press **Ctrl** +click ▶ (⌘ +click ▶ on a Mac).

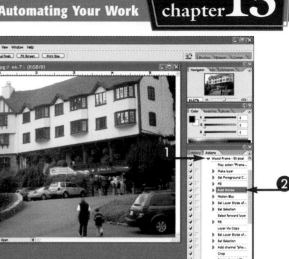

Photoshop executes the selected command, but no commands before or after it.

In this example, the selected command adds noise to the image.

 TIP

How do I assign a special key command to an action?

Click ▣ to open the Actions palette menu, and then click **Action Options** to open the Action Options dialog box. Select a key command from the Function Key menu. Then, to perform an action on an image, press the function key. You may want to avoid assigning function keys that are already associated with a command. To view assigned key commands, click **Edit** and then **Keyboard Shortcuts**.

Batch Process by Using an Action

You can apply an action to multiple images automatically with Photoshop's Batch command. The command is a great timesaver for tasks such as optimizing large numbers of digital photos.

Batch Process by Using an Action

1 Place all the images you want to apply an action to in a source folder.

2 Create a destination folder in which to save your batch-processed files.

Note: *To work with folders, see your operating system's documentation.*

3 In Photoshop, click **File**.

4 Click **Automate**.

5 Click **Batch**.

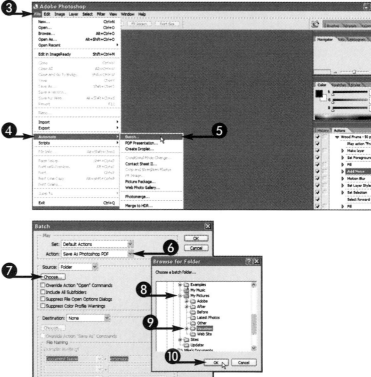

The Batch dialog box opens.

6 Click here and select an action to apply.

7 Click **Choose**.

The Browse for Folder (Choose a batch folder on a Mac) dialog box appears.

8 In Windows, click the plus button (⊞) to open folders on your computer (⊞ changes to ⊟).

9 Click the folder containing your images.

10 Click **OK** (**Choose** on a Mac).

⑪ Click here and select **Folder**.

⑫ Click **Choose** and repeat steps **8** and **9** to select the folder where you want your batch-processed files to be saved.

● You can specify a naming scheme for saving the batch-processed files.

⑬ Click **OK** (**Choose** on a Mac).

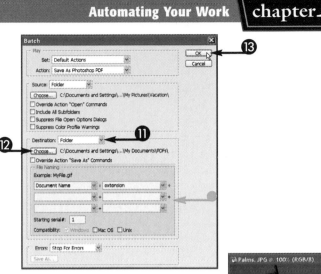

Photoshop opens each image in the specified folder one at a time, applies the action, and then saves the files in the destination directory.

How can I change the mode — such as RGB Color or Grayscale — of an image during a batch process depending on its current mode?

When you record the original action, click **File**, **Automate**, and then **Conditional Mode Change**. A dialog box appears and asks you to specify the source modes that you want to switch as well as a target mode. When the action is run as a batch process, images that are of a selected source mode are converted.

How do I batch process using an action in Mac OS X?

You do this very much like a Windows user would, but with the Open dialog box instead of with the Browse for Folder dialog box. When you click **Choose** in step **7**, the Open-style dialog box appears. Using the file browser in the center of the dialog box, locate the source and destination folders for your batch-processed images.

Create a
Contact Sheet

Photoshop can automatically create a digital version of a photographer's contact sheet. Useful for keeping a hard-copy record of your digital images, contact sheets consist of miniature versions of images.

For information about printing a contact sheet after you create it, see Chapter 15.

Create a Contact Sheet

① Place the images that you want on the contact sheet in a folder.

Note: To work with folders, see your operating system's documentation.

② Click **File**.

③ Click **Automate**.

④ Click **Contact Sheet II**.

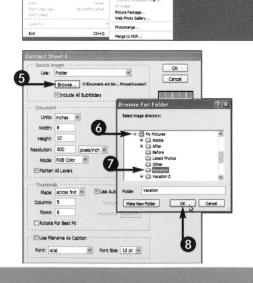

The Contact Sheet II dialog box appears.

⑤ Click **Browse** (**Choose** on a Mac).

The Browse for Folder (Select image directory on a Mac) dialog box appears.

⑥ In Windows, click ⊞ to open folders on your computer (⊞ changes to ⊟).

Note: See the section "Batch Process by Using an Action" to choose a folder on a Mac.

⑦ Click the folder containing your images.

⑧ Click **OK**.

⑨ Set the contact sheet properties.

You can set the contact sheet size and resolution, the order and number of columns and rows in the sheet, and the caption font and font size.

● Photoshop displays a preview of the layout.

⑩ Click **OK**.

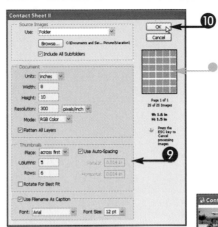

Photoshop creates and displays your contact sheet.

If there are more images than can fit on a single page, Photoshop creates multiple contact sheets.

Note: To save your contact sheet, see Chapter 14.

TIP

How do I make the thumbnail images larger on my contact sheet?

Paper size and the number of rows and columns automatically determine the size of the thumbnails. To increase the thumbnail size, type a smaller number of rows and columns for the sheet in the Columns and Rows boxes in the Contact Sheet II dialog box.

Create a Picture Package

You can automatically create a one-page layout with one or more selected images at various sizes using the Picture Package command. You may find this useful when you want to print pictures for friends, family, or associates.

For information about printing a picture package after you create it, see Chapter 15.

Create a Picture Package

1. Click **File**.
2. Click **Automate**.
3. Click **Picture Package**.

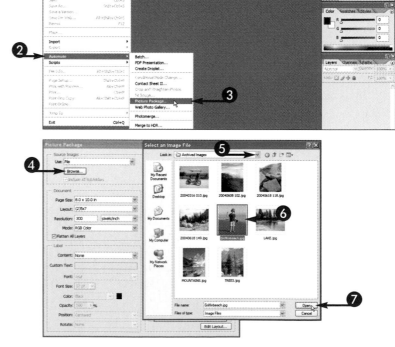

The Picture Package dialog box appears.

4. Click **Browse** (**Choose** on a Mac).

The Select an Image File dialog box appears.

5. In Windows, click here and select the folder that contains the image file.

Note: *See the section "Batch Process by Using an Action" to choose a folder on a Mac.*

6. Click the image file.
7. Click **Open**.

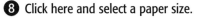

8 Click here and select a paper size.

9 Click here and select a layout.

● A preview of the layout appears.

You can click an individual thumbnail to change the image file displayed in that position.

You can also change the resolution and color mode in the dialog box.

10 Click **OK**.

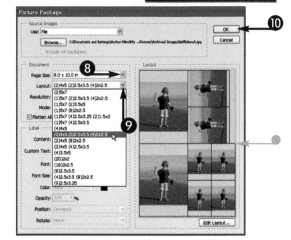

Photoshop constructs the picture package step by step, and then opens a new image window with the picture package inside it.

Note: To save your picture package, see Chapter 14.

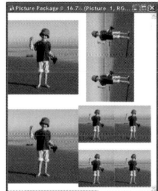

 TIPS

How do I label my picture package?

At the bottom of the Picture Package dialog box, you can choose labels such as copyright or caption information, the image file name, or custom text that you define. To set copyright and caption information for an image, see Chapter 14.

How can I create my own custom picture package layout?

In the bottom-right corner of the Picture Package dialog box, click **Edit Layout**. A Picture Package Edit Layout dialog box appears, enabling you to edit an existing layout or create a new one.

Create a Web Photo Gallery

You can have Photoshop create a photo gallery Web site that showcases your images. Photoshop not only sizes and optimizes your image files for the site, but also creates the Web pages that display the images, and links those pages together.

After you create your photo gallery, you can use an FTP program such as WS FTP in Windows or RBrowserLite on a Mac to upload your images to a Web server.

Create a Web Photo Gallery

① Place all the images you want to feature in your Web photo gallery in a folder.

② Create a separate folder where Photoshop can save all the image files and HTML files necessary for your gallery.

Note: To work with folders, see your operating system's documentation.

③ Click **File**.

④ Click **Automate**.

⑤ Click **Web Photo Gallery**.

⑥ Click here and select a photo gallery style.

● Photoshop displays a preview of the style.

⑦ Click here and select **Banner**.

You can select other options to further customize your gallery.

⑧ Type a site name for your Web gallery pages.

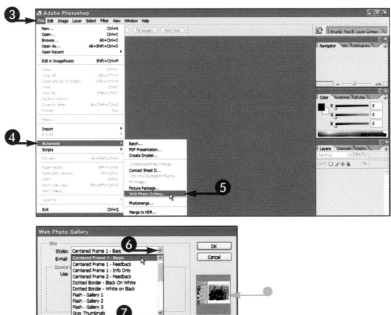

⑨ Click **Browse** (**Choose** on a Mac).

The Browse For Folder (Select image directory on a Mac) dialog box appears.

⑩ Select the folder containing your images.

⑪ Click **OK**.

⑫ Click **Destination** and repeat steps **10** and **11** to specify the folder in which to save your gallery.

⑬ Click **OK** in the Web Photo Gallery dialog box.

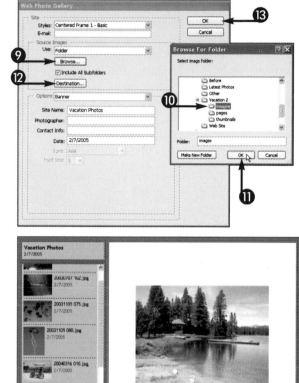

Photoshop opens each image in the specified folder, creates versions for the photo gallery, and generates the necessary HTML.

After the processing is complete, Photoshop opens the default Web browser on your computer and displays the home page of the gallery.

● You can click a thumbnail to see a larger version of the image.

TIPS

How can I allow viewers the option of sending me feedback from my Web photo gallery pages?

In the Web photo gallery dialog box, type your e-mail address in the E-mail field. Then, in the Styles menu, select a gallery style that includes "Feedback" in the style name. When Photoshop builds the Web photo gallery, it includes an option on the pages that allows viewers to send feedback about the gallery photos. You can check your e-mail to read the feedback.

How can I create a photo gallery based on Flash instead of HTML?

You can create Flash-based photo galleries by choosing one of the Flash styles in the Web Photo Gallery dialog box. To view Flash-based galleries, your browser must have the Flash plug-in installed. Flash-based galleries include control buttons in the lower-right corner that enable you to display the images sequentially as a slide show.

Create a Panoramic Image

You can use the Photomerge feature in Photoshop to stitch several images together into a single panoramic image. This enables you to capture more scenery than is usually possible in a regular photograph.

Create a Panoramic Image

① Click **File**.

② Click **Automate**.

③ Click **Photomerge**.

The Photomerge dialog box appears.

④ Click **Browse**.

The Open dialog box appears.

Note: For more information about the Open dialog box on a Mac, see Chapter 1.

⑤ Click here and select the folder that contains the images you want to merge.

⑥ Press Ctrl (⌘ on a Mac) and then click the images you want to merge into a panoramic image.

⑦ Click **Open**.

● The file names of the images appear in the Source Files list.

⑧ Click **OK** to build the panoramic image.

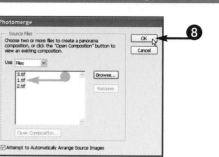

● Photoshop attempts to merge the images into a single panoramic image.

● Thumbnails of the images that it cannot merge appear in a lightbox area.

● You can click and drag 🔲 to zoom the panoramic image in and out.

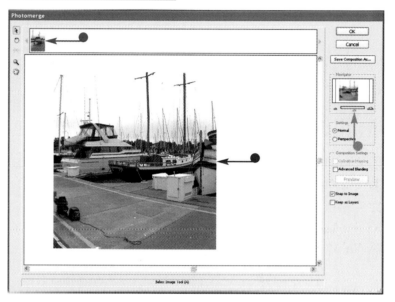

TIP

How can I create photos that merge successfully?

To merge photos successfully, you need to align and overlap them. Here are a few hints. For more tips, see the Photoshop Help documentation.

● Use a tripod to keep your photos level with one another.

● Experiment with the **Perspective** setting in the Photomerge dialog box. This setting can be useful if you use a tripod to shoot your photos.

● Refrain from using lenses, such as fisheye lenses, that distort your photos.

● Shoot your photos so that they overlap at least 30%.

continued

The Photomerge dialog box enables you to interactively align the images that make up your panorama.

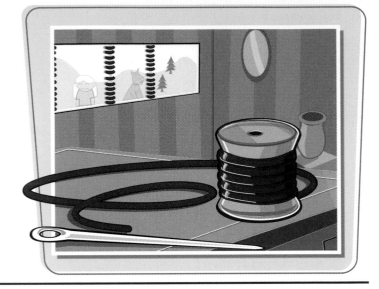

Create a Panoramic Image (continued)

⑨ Click the **Select Image** tool (🖾).

⑩ Click and drag an image from the lightbox to the work area.

⑪ Place the image so that it lines up with its neighboring image in the panorama.

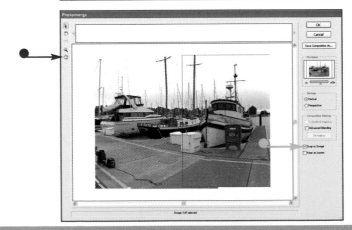

● If you select **Snap to Image** (☐ changes to ☑), Photoshop tries to merge the image edges after you click and drag.

● You can use the **Move View** tool (🖑) to adjust the placement of the entire panoramic image inside the main window.

⑫ Repeat steps **9** to **11** for any other images in the lightbox so that they overlap and match one another.

● You can click the **Rotate Image** tool (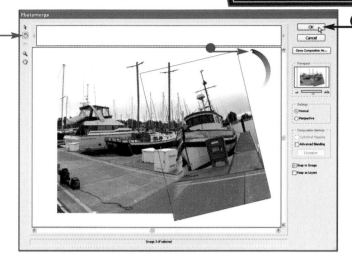) and then click and drag with it to align image seams that are not level with one another.

⑬ Click **OK**.

⑬

Photoshop merges the images and opens the panorama in a new image window.

Note: *To save the panorama, see Chapter 14. To print the panorama, see Chapter 15.*

TIP

How do I apply perspective to my panorama?

❶ In the Photomerge dialog box, click the **Perspective** option (○ changes to ◉).

❷ Click the **Vanishing Point** tool (⊡).

❸ Click the part of the image that will serve as the focal point for your panorama.

When you apply this option, Photoshop warps the area next to the vanishing point slightly to provide the correct perspective.

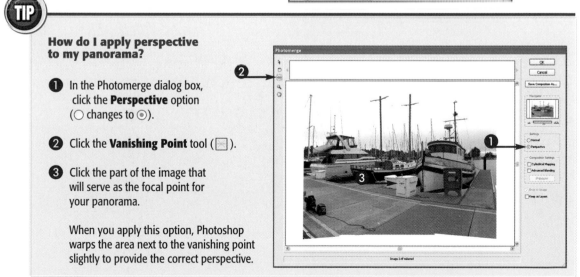

Convert File Types

You can quickly and easily convert images from one file type to another in Photoshop using the Image Processor script. This makes it easy to convert a collection of TIFF files to the JPEG format for posting on the Web.

The Image Processor script allows you to convert to the JPEG, PSD, and TIFF file formats only.

Convert File Types

1 Place the images that you want to convert in a folder.

Note: To work with folders, see your operating system's documentation.

2 Click **File**.

3 Click **Scripts**.

4 Click **Image Processor**.

The Image Processor dialog box appears.

5 Click **Select Folder**.

The Browse for Folder (Select image directory on a Mac) dialog box appears.

6 In Windows, click ⊞ to open folders on your computer (⊞ changes to ⊟).

7 Click the folder containing your images.

8 Click **OK**.

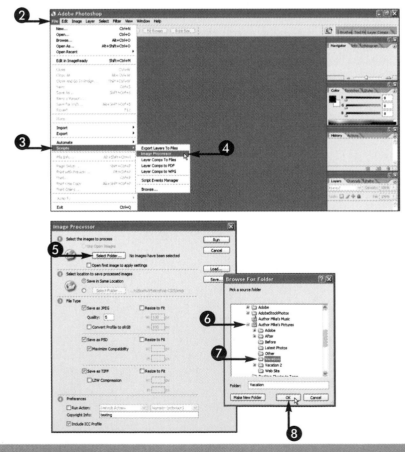

⑨ Specify where you want your processed images to be saved.

⑩ Specify an image format to save the images as (☐ changes to ☑).

● If you choose JPEG, you can also specify a quality setting from 1 to 10; the higher the quality setting, the larger the resulting file size.

You can click multiple format check boxes; Photoshop saves a separate image file for each format selected.

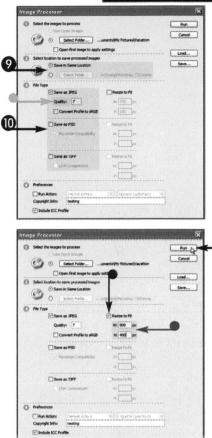

● You can optionally click **Resize to Fit** (☐ changes to ☑), and type a new width and height.

Photoshop will resize the images before saving.

● You can specify the dimensions of the resized images.

Note: *Photoshop keeps the proportions of any resized images unchanged.*

⑪ Click **Run**.

Photoshop processes the images.

TIPS

How can I quickly add the same copyright information to multiple images?

In the Image Processor dialog box, type the copyright information into the Copyright Info field. Photoshop adds the information to the processed images. To view the copyright information of an image in Photoshop, open the image and click **File** and then **File Info**.

How can I save my Image Processor settings so I can use them again later?

Click **Save** in the Image Processor dialog box. Another dialog box opens enabling you to save the settings as an XML file. To load previously saved settings, click **Load** in the Image Processor dialog box.

CHAPTER

14

Saving Images

Do you want to save your images for use later, or so that you can use them in another application or on the Web? This chapter shows you how.

Save in the Photoshop Format

You can save your image in Photoshop's native image format. This format enables you to retain multiple layers in your image, if it has them. This is the best format in which to save your images if you still need to edit them.

The Photoshop PDF and TIFF file formats also support multiple layers.

① Click **File**.

② Click **Save As**.

● If you have named and saved your image previously and just want to save changes, you can click **File** and then **Save**.

The Save As dialog box appears.

③ Click **Use Adobe Dialog**.

Photoshop switches to a dialog box specific to Adobe applications.

④ Click here and click a folder in which to save the image file.

⑤ Click here and select the Photoshop file format.

⑥ Type a name for the image file.

Photoshop automatically assigns a .psd extension.

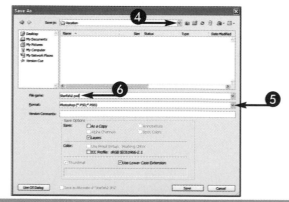

- To save a copy of the file and keep the existing file open, you can click **As a Copy** (changes to).

- To merge the multiple layers of your image into one layer, you can click **Layers** (changes to).

7 Click **Save**.

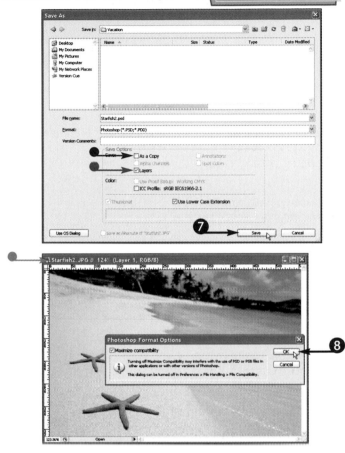

The Photoshop Format Options dialog box appears.

8 Click **OK** to make sure your image is compatible with other applications.

Photoshop saves the image file.

- The name of the file appears in the image's title bar.

TIP

What are the shortcuts for saving an image in Photoshop?
You can use several keyboard commands for saving your image:

Command	Windows Shortcut	Mac Shortcut
Save	Ctrl + S	⌘ + S
Save As...	Shift + Ctrl + S	Shift + ⌘ + S
Save for Web	Alt + Shift + Ctrl + S	Option + Shift + ⌘ + S

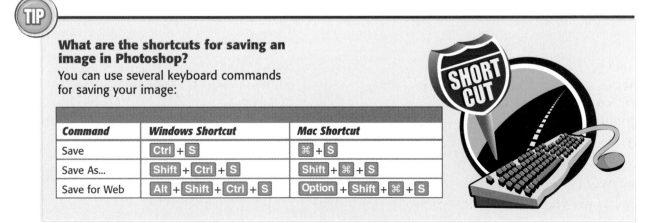

Save an Image for Use in Another Application

You can save your image in a format that can be opened and used in other imaging or page layout applications. TIFF (Tagged Image File Format) and EPS (Encapsulated PostScript) are standard printing formats that many applications on both Windows and Macintosh platforms support.

BMP – bitmap – is a popular Windows image format, and PICT is a Macintosh image format.

Note that most image formats – with the exception of the Photoshop PSD, Photoshop PDF, and TIFF formats – do not support layers.

Save an Image for Use in Another Application

① Click **File**.

② Click **Save As**.

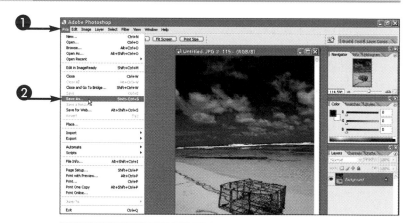

The Save As dialog box appears.

③ In Windows, click here and select a folder in which to save the image file.

④ In Windows, click here and select a file format.

If you are saving a multilayer image and select a file format that does not support layers, an alert icon appears. Photoshop saves a flattened copy of the image.

Note: See the section "Save in the Photoshop Format" to save a multilayer image. For more about flattening, see Chapter 8.

⑤ Type a file name.

Photoshop automatically assigns an appropriate extension for the file format, such as .tif for TIFF or .eps for EPS.

⑥ Click **Save**.

Photoshop displays a dialog box of options specific to the format in which you are saving – EPS format in this example.

⑦ Click **OK**.

Photoshop saves the image.

If a flattened copy was saved, the original multilayer version remains in the image window.

TIPS

How do I choose a file format for my image?

You should choose the format based on how you want to use the image. If it is a multilayered image and you want to preserve the layers, save it as a Photoshop file. If you want to use the image in word processing or page layout applications, save it as a TIFF or EPS file. If you want to use the image on the Web, save it as a JPEG, PNG, or GIF file. For more information on file formats, see the rest of this chapter as well as Photoshop's documentation.

What are some popular page layout programs with which I might use images?

Adobe InDesign and QuarkXPress are two popular page layout programs. They let you combine text and images to create brochures, magazines, and other printed media. You can import TIFF and EPS files saved in Photoshop into both programs.

Save a JPEG for the Web

You can save a file in the JPEG —
Joint Photographic Experts Group —
format and publish it on the Web.
JPEG is the preferred file format for
saving photographic images.

Photoshop saves JPEG images at 72 dpi.

Save a JPEG for the Web

① Click **File**.

② Click **Save for Web**.

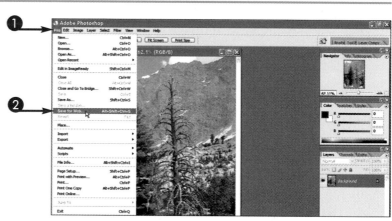

The Save For Web dialog box appears.

③ Click the **2-Up** tab.

④ Click here and select **JPEG**.

⑤ Click here and select a quality setting.

● Alternatively, you can select a numeric quality
setting from **0** (low quality) to **100** (high quality).

The higher the quality, the larger the resulting
file size.

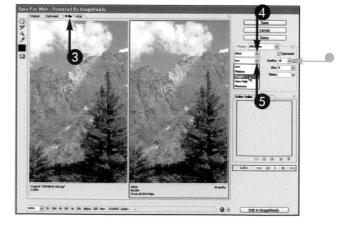

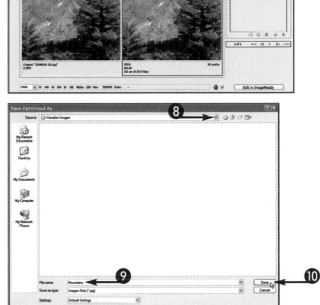

⑥ Check that the file quality and size are acceptable in the preview window.

● You can use the **Hand** tool (🖐) to move the image in the preview window.

● You can use the **Zoom** tool (🔍) to magnify the image in the preview window.

⑦ Click **Save**.

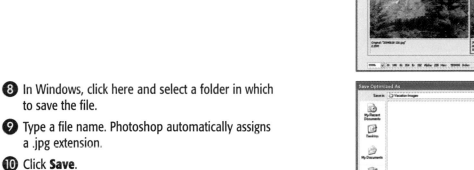

⑧ In Windows, click here and select a folder in which to save the file.

⑨ Type a file name. Photoshop automatically assigns a .jpg extension.

⑩ Click **Save**.

The original image file remains open in Photoshop.

TIPS

What is image compression?

Image compression involves using mathematical techniques to reduce the amount of information required to describe an image. This results in smaller file sizes, which is important when transmitting information on the Web. Some compression schemes, such as JPEG, involve some loss in quality due to the compression, but the loss is usually negligible compared to the file size savings.

What file size should I make my Web images?

If a large portion of your audience uses dial-up modems to view your Web pages, keep your images small enough so that total page size — which includes all the images on the page plus the HTML file — is below 50K. You can check the file size and the download speed of an image at the bottom of the Save For Web preview pane. To change an image's file size and download speed, you can adjust the quality and color settings in the Save For Web dialog box. See the section "Save a GIF for the Web" for details.

Save a GIF for the Web

You can save a file as a GIF — Graphics Interchange Format — and publish it on the Web. The GIF format is good for saving illustrations that have a lot of solid color. The format supports a maximum of 256 colors.

Photoshop saves GIF images at 72 dpi.

Save a GIF for the Web

① Click **File**.

② Click **Save for Web**.

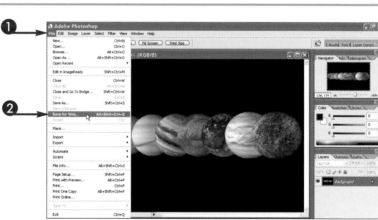

The Save For Web dialog box appears.

③ Click the **2-Up** tab.

④ Click here and select **GIF**.

⑤ Click here and select the number of colors to include in the image.

GIF allows a maximum of 256 colors.

● You can click here to choose the algorithm that Photoshop uses to select the GIF colors.

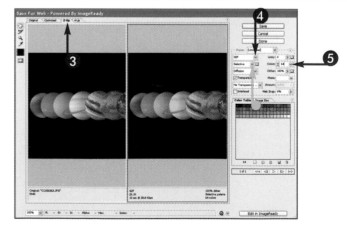

6 Check that the file quality and size are acceptable in the preview window.

● You can use to move the image in the preview window.

● You can use 🔍 to magnify the image in the preview window.

7 Click **Save**.

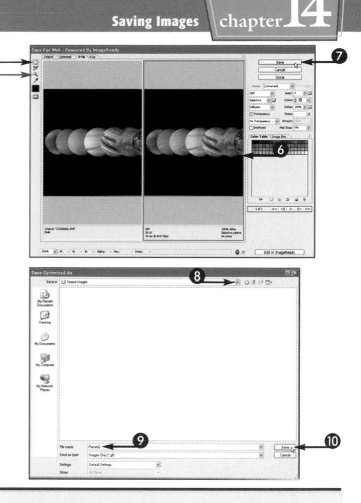

8 In Windows, click here and select a folder in which to save the file.

On a Mac, use the Where pop-up menu or the File Browser to select a folder.

9 Type a file name. Photoshop automatically assigns a .gif extension.

10 Click **Save**.

The original image file remains open in Photoshop.

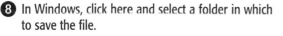

TIPS

How do I minimize the file sizes of my GIF images?

The most important factor in creating small GIFs is limiting the number of colors in the final image. GIF files are limited to 256 colors or fewer. In images that have just a few solid colors, you can often reduce the total number of colors to 16 or even 8 without any noticeable reduction in quality. See step **5** in this section to set the number of colors in your GIF images.

What are Web-safe colors?

They are the 216 colors that are available to browsers running on 256-color monitors. If you want to ensure your GIF images look the way you expect on such monitors, you can select the **Restrictive (Web) palette** setting in the Save For Web dialog box. Photoshop converts the colors in your image to those that are Web safe. Today, the vast majority of monitors can display thousands or millions of colors at a time, so choosing Web-safe colors is less important than it was in the past.

You can include transparency in files saved in the GIF file format. The transparent pixels do not show up on Web pages, allowing the background behind the image to show through.

Because Photoshop Background layers cannot contain transparent pixels, you need to work with layers other than the Background layer to create transparent GIFs. See Chapter 8 for more about layers.

Save a GIF with Transparency

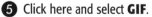

1 With a selection tool, select the area that you want to make transparent.

Note: See Chapter 4 for more about using the selection tools.

2 Press Delete to delete the pixels.

Photoshop replaces the deleted pixels with a checkerboard pattern.

3 Click **File**.

4 Click **Save for Web**.

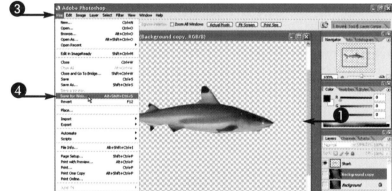

The Save For Web dialog box appears.

5 Click here and select **GIF**.

6 Click the **Transparency** option to retain transparency in the saved file (changes to).

7 Click here and select the number of colors to include in the image.

GIF allows a maximum of 256 colors.

8 Click **Save**.

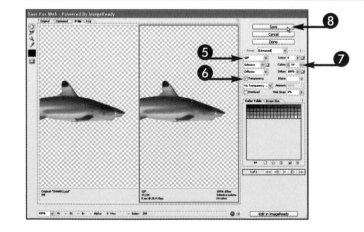

9 In Windows, click here and select a folder in which to save the file.

Mac users should use the Where pop-up menu or the File Browser to select a folder.

10 Type a name for the file.

Photoshop automatically assigns a .gif extension.

11 Click **Save**.

In this example, the image has been added to a Web page and opened in a Web browser.

The transparency causes the Web page background to show through around the edges of the object.

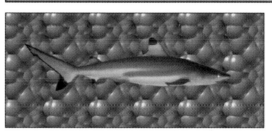

TIP

Does the JPEG format support transparency?

No. JPEG, the other popular image format for the Web, does not support transparency. However, you can simulate transparency in a JPEG image by surrounding elements in the image with a color that matches the intended background.

Add Descriptive and Copyright Information

You can store title, author, caption, and copyright information with your saved image. You may find this useful if you plan on publishing the images online.

Some image-editing applications — such as Photoshop — can detect copyright information in an image and display it when the image is opened.

Add Descriptive and Copyright Information

① Click **File**.

② Click **File Info**.

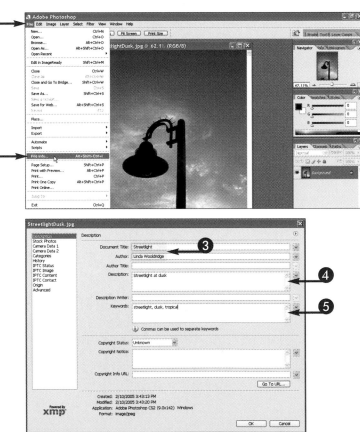

The File Info dialog box appears.

③ Type title and author information for the image.

④ Type a description for the image.

⑤ Type keywords for the image.

6 Click here and select a **Copyright Status**.

7 Type the copyright information for the image.

8 Click **OK**.

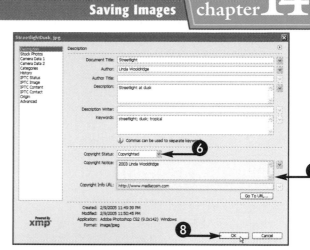

● If you marked the image as copyrighted, Photoshop places a copyright symbol in the title bar.

To save the copyrighted image, see the other sections in this chapter.

TIP

How do I view information about a photo taken with a digital camera?

Information about photos taken with a digital camera can be accessed in the File Info dialog box. You can view the information by clicking the **Camera Data 1** or **Camera Data 2** category in the dialog box. The information includes the model of the camera, the date and time the photo was shot, and the image dimensions.

Save a Sliced Image

You can save an image that has been sliced with the Slice Select tool. Photoshop saves the slices as different images and also saves an HTML file that organizes the slices into a Web page. Slices enable you to save some parts of an image as GIF and others as JPEG. This can result in a smaller overall file size for the image.

For more information about using the Slice tool, see Chapter 4.

Save a Sliced Image

① Open your sliced image.

② Click **File**.

③ Click **Save for Web**.

The Save For Web dialog box appears.

④ Click the **Slice Select** tool (🔲).

⑤ Click one of the image slices to select it.

⑥ Specify the optimization settings for the slice.

⑦ Repeat steps **5** and **6** for each of the slices.

⑧ Click **Save**.

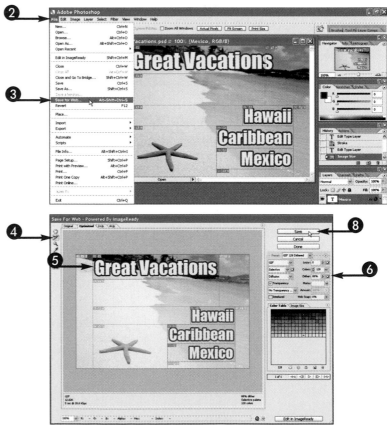

⑨ Select a folder in which to save the files; in Windows, click here.

On a Mac, use the Where pop-up menu or the File Browser.

⑩ In Windows, click here and select **HTML and Images** as the file type.

On a Mac, click the Format ⬚.

⑪ Type the name of the HTML file that will organize the slices.

Photoshop saves the images by appending slice numbers to the original image name.

● To change the naming scheme, you can click here and select **Other**.

⑫ Click **Save**.

You can access the HTML and image files in the folder that you specified in step **9**.

● The image files are saved in a separate images subfolder.

● To view the Web page, you can double-click the HTML file.

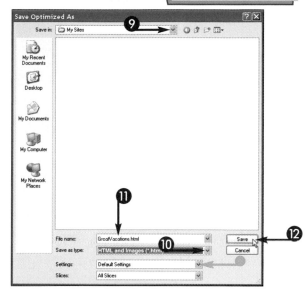

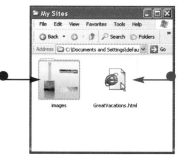

TIP

How do I publish my Web page online?

After you create a Web page by saving your sliced Photoshop image, you can make the page available online by transferring the HTML and image files to a Web server using an FTP program. Most people arrange for Web server access through an Internet service provider, or ISP. Mac OS X users have the Apache Web server built into their computer's operating system.

CHAPTER 15

Printing Images

Printing enables you to save the digital imagery you create in Photoshop in hard copy form. Photoshop can print to black-and-white or color printers.

You can print your Photoshop image in color or black and white on a PC using an inkjet, laser, or other type of printer.

Print on a PC

① Make sure the layers you want to print are visible.

Note: *An Eye icon ( ) means that a layer is visible. For more about layers, see Chapter 8.*

② Click **File**.

③ Click **Print**.

If your image is larger than your printer paper, a warning appears. Click **Proceed**.

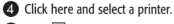

The Print dialog box appears.

④ Click here and select a printer.

⑤ Click to select the number of copies.

⑥ Click **Properties**.

The Properties dialog box appears.

The options available will vary with the type of printer.

⑦ Click the **Size is** ⊡ and select a paper size.

⑧ Click the **Type is** ⊡ and select the type of paper on which to print.

⑨ Click the **Print Quality** ⊡ and select the quality at which to print.

⑩ Click the **Basics** tab.

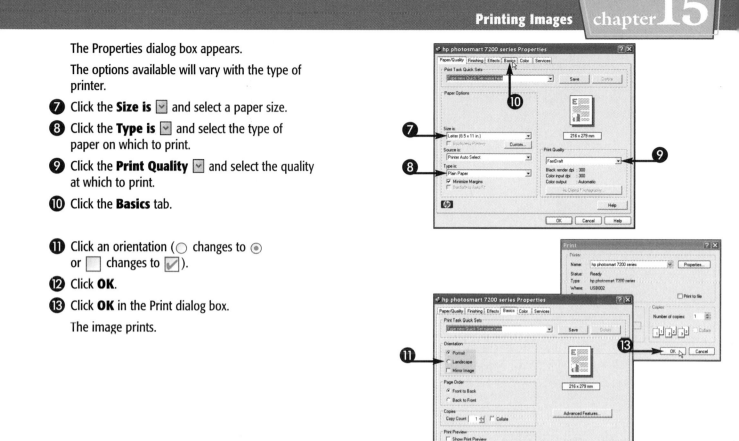

⑪ Click an orientation (○ changes to ⊙ or ☐ changes to ☑).

⑫ Click **OK**.

⑬ Click **OK** in the Print dialog box.

The image prints.

TIPS

Is there a shortcut for quickly printing one copy of an image?

To print your image on the currently selected printer using the current print settings, click **File** and then **Print One Copy**. This skips the Print and Properties dialog boxes.

Is there an easy way to resize an image for print?

Photoshop offers a Resize Image Wizard that prepares your image for either print or online use. Click **Help** and then **Resize Image**. The dialog box that appears helps you control the dimensions, resolution, and resulting image quality. For information on resizing using different methods, see the section "Preview a Printout," or Chapter 3.

You can print your Photoshop image in color or black and white on a Macintosh using an inkjet, laser, or other type of printer.

Print on a Macintosh

SET UP THE PAGE

1 Make sure that the layers you want to print are visible.

Note: An 👁 *means that a layer is visible. For more about layers, see Chapter 8.*

2 Click **File**.

3 Click **Page Setup**.

The Page Setup dialog box appears.

4 Click 🔽 and select a paper size.

5 Click an orientation button (🔳, 🔳, or 🔳).

● You can type a value to increase or decrease the printed size on the page.

6 Click **OK**.

PRINT THE IMAGE

7 Click **File**.

8 Click **Print**.

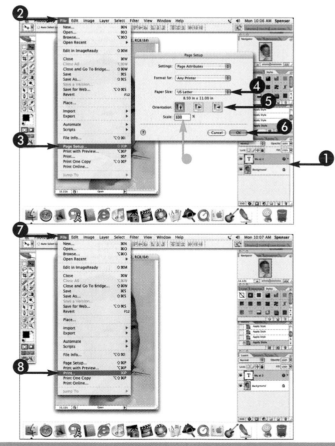

The Print dialog box appears.

9 Click ![icon] and select a printer.

10 Type the number of copies to print.

11 Click the range of pages you want to print
(○ changes to ⊙) and type a range, if necessary.

12 Click **Copies & Pages** and then click **Print Settings**.

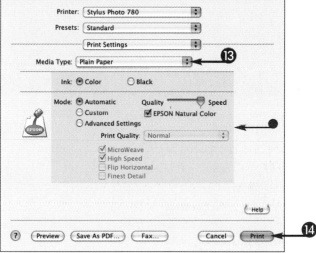

The printer-specific settings pane appears.

13 Click the **Media Type** ![icon] and choose the type of paper on which to print

● You can specify any other printer-specific settings.

14 Click **Print**.

The image prints.

TIPS

What is halftoning?

In grayscale printing, *halftoning* is the process by which a printer creates the appearance of different shades of gray using only black ink. If you look closely at a grayscale image printed on most black-and-white laser printers, you see that the image consists of tiny, differently sized dots. Larger dots produce the darker gray areas of the image, and smaller dots produce the lighter gray areas.

How do I re-create a group of printer settings on the Mac?

When you have all the options you want specified for a print job, you can click the **Presets** pop-up menu, choose **Save As,** and give the settings a name. Henceforth, whenever you print, those settings will be available in the Presets pop-up menu as a single entry.

Preview a Printout

You can preview your printout — as well as adjust the size and positioning of your printed image — in a special dialog box in Photoshop. Previewing lets you check and adjust your work before putting ink on paper.

Preview a Printout

① Make sure the layers you want to print are visible.

Note: An Eye icon ( ) means that a layer is visible. For more about layers, see Chapter 8.

② Click **File**.

③ Click **Print with Preview**.

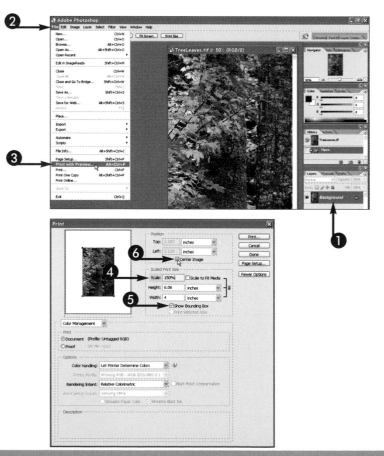

The Print dialog box appears.

④ Type a percentage in the Scale box to shrink or enlarge the image.

⑤ To reposition and resize the image, click the **Show Bounding Box** check box (changes to).

⑥ Click **Center Image** to allow for the repositioning of the image (changes to).

⑦ Click and drag in the image window to reposition the image on the page.

● You can position your image precisely by typing values in the Top and Left fields.

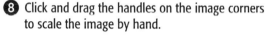

⑧ Click and drag the handles on the image corners to scale the image by hand.

⑨ Click **Print**.

The image prints.

TIPS

How can I maximize the size of my image on the printed page?

In the Print dialog box, you can click the **Scale to Fit Media** option (☐ changes to ☑) to scale the image to the maximum size given the current print settings.

How can I print just a selected part of an image?

Before performing the Print with Preview, select a part of your image with the **Rectangular Marquee** tool. Click the **Print Selected Area** option (☐ changes to ☑) in the Print dialog box. This feature does not work with areas selected using the **Elliptical Marquee**, **Lasso**, or **Magic Wand** tools. For more on these tools, see Chapters 4 and 5.

Index

Index